18 Steps to Win a Local Election

by Robert D. Butler

An **ICAN** Book

Independent Candidate Action Network

ISBN 13: 978-0-9820141-7-2
ISBN 10:0-9820141-7-1

Published in 2009 in the United States by
Adsum Press, a division of
Woolstrum Publishing House LLC.

www.adsumpress.com
www.indyaction.org
www.governmentbasics.com

Printed in the United States of America
on acid-free paper.
All trademarks are owned by
their respective companies.

16 15 14 13 12 11 10 09 08 07 06 05 04 03 02 01

For all those who work towards greater liberty
and the restoration of the Republic.

About the Author

Robert Butler is the Executive Director of the Libertarian Party of Texas. He was born just outside Valley Forge, Pennsylvania in 1973 and maintains his close connection to those fateful days of 1776.

He began his political career in high school when he became the Military and Veteran Affairs Intern for U.S. Senator Connie Mack of Florida in 1989. He believed that only a limited government could allow people the freedom to prosper and find success and happiness. Robert studied at the Elliot School of International Relations at George Washington University and the George Washington University Graduate School of Political Management from 1991 to 1995. During those college years, he worked for U.S. Representative Porter Goss, the Republican National Committee, and a number of local candidates from his hometown in Florida.

After the Republicans were swept into power in 1995, Robert realized that the Republican Party was not committed to dramatically shrinking the size and scope of government. He left politics completely and traveled extensively in the countries of Taiwan, Hong Kong, and Mexico. He worked as an English teacher and eventually opened his own language school in the Yucatan. While outside the U.S., he witnessed the first democratic elections for President in Taiwan and Mexico. Both countries had been dominated by single party rule and had courageous minor political parties that overcame great odds.

After the tragedy of September 11 and the policies of George W. Bush thereafter, Robert decided to return to the U.S. The Libertarian Party had become much stronger and influential in the late 1990's. He felt he had the skills and experience to help the party grow. Robert served as Development Coordinator for the Libertarian Party of Indiana. He was the full-time Executive Director of the Libertarian Party of Ohio for two years. He also volunteered his service as secretary and chair of the Libertarian Party of Ohio. In January 2009, he was asked to replace Wes Benedict as the Executive Director of the Libertarian Party of Texas.

Robert is married and has three children. He lives near Austin, Texas.

Contents

Foreword

I have run for office three times. I lost once, won twice. I have also presided as state chair of the Libertarian Party of Texas for the past six years as we have placed over three hundred candidates on the ballot. That does not make me Karl Rove or James Carville, but I have learned from my experience.

If you do not have experience running for office or working on a campaign, this book is for you. This book does have some focus on candidates running as Libertarians, but it can be applied to anyone running for office. The principles of running a good campaign are universal, but there are unique challenges when you are running against incumbents and larger political parties.

Also, do not feel that you have to do everything in this book. If you have the resources to run a complete campaign, go for it. However, for some of the smaller races, you can still win by focusing on the most important aspects conveyed in this book and tailoring the campaign to the size of your effort.

Another aspect of campaigning is that you don't have to win to win. That may be paradoxical, but there is great benefit in running for office even when the odds are against you. By running an effective campaign, you can raise issues, influence policy, and possibly be a factor in how the vote swings from one candidate to another. Playing a "kingmaker" role is a very powerful way to influence policy even if you are not the winning candidate. This book will help make the most of your efforts to be a significant player in the election.

If you are serious about influencing policy and making an impact, I highly recommend you boldly try running for office. If you run for office or want to help with a campaign, I highly recommend this book.

Yours in Liberty,

Patrick J Dixon
Libertarian Party National Committee, At-large Member Chair,
Libertarian Party of Texas (www.LPTexas.org)

Introduction

If you go through each of the steps, you will have a solid foundation for winning a local campaign. This handbook was created to help candidates and volunteers win more elections and fight more effective campaigns. It can help you bring order to your campaigns by systematically guiding you through the campaign process.

Please keep in mind that this book was primarily written for Independents, minor party candidates, and major party reformers. For brevity, I refer to all these candidates as Independents.

The first pages of most campaign books will solemnly advise you to run as a mainstream Republican or Democrat in any partisan race. They predict that running as an Independent or (heaven forbid) a minor party candidate will be an uphill battle, and that you will probably lose. Until recently, this advice was fairly accurate. Even now, running as an Independent may be more of a liability than an asset. Nevertheless, thousands of Independent candidates now run for office every year and over eight hundred minor party officials currently sit in public office.

Countless Independents have followed the advice of these campaign books and decided to choose a party, whether it matched their philosophy of government or not. Numerous factors are taken into account in deciding whether to run as a Republican or Democrat. These factors include: the relative strength or weakness of the party in their district, the opinions of their friends and family, the financial strength of their local parties, local community issues, the support of their contributors and volunteers, and their personal beliefs.

The strength of your local party's organization is an important factor in deciding how you will run for office. Clearly, an organized party is more likely to be of assistance in your efforts to win. The local party has decades of experience. Past candidates can instruct you on the specifics of how to win in your community and help you steer clear of obstacles. They will have helpful contacts with the press, financial contributors, a list of volunteers, and perhaps a paid staff.

The local party may even be able to "guarantee" your victory through its proven model of success and support among the voters.

Your friends, coworkers, and family may even be members or activists in the Republican or Democratic parties. It is difficult to turn aside the social pressure to follow suit. Independents and minor party candidates are often ridiculed or easily dismissed as unimportant distractions from the "real race." This kind of public rejection can be hurtful and may influence your relationship with your friends and family.

Fundraising is the most important aspect of any campaign. It takes money to get a candidate's message before the public and create a professional appearance for your campaign. The major parties are very helpful in raising money. They possess long lists of local contributors who may be willing to give your campaign money simply because of your party identification. Most campaigns and the issues they champion are driven by the need to raise large sums of money. Having an established financial network takes pressure off the campaign and the candidate.

Most local political parties will be well known for championing specific local issues including taxes, bonds, bike paths, redevelopment, infrastructure, housing, and schools. You may find that a particular issue strongly resonates with your community's voters and that one of the major parties has staked a claim on that issue. This kind of party branding can often make your campaign very emotional for your neighborhood. It may even create an impossible situation for any other party's candidate to win unless he or she can successfully defuse the issue.

Sadly, personal philosophy usually takes a back seat to the candidate's desire to win office. Most candidates are able to shoehorn their personal politics into one of the major parties. They believe in cutting taxes so they become a Republican. They believe in helping the disadvantaged so they become a Democrat. They may just follow in the footsteps of their family tradition. They go along with what they've been taught in school. They may even switch parties to give themselves a better chance at success.

Why should you run as an Independent or minor party candidate? Independents are marked by a strong desire to follow their true political and personal beliefs. They often believe that government is not the most efficient method of achieving public goals. They believe that individual liberty and personal responsibility are the answers to our social ills. They disagree with Republicans when they increase spending through borrowing money. They disagree with Democrats who try to use government to solve all of our personal problems. Independents' disagreements with the major parties are so strong that they feel there is no place for them within the two-party system that governs this country.

Major Party or Minor Party?

You may consider joining one of the major parties. After all, you may be able to "change the party from within." There are certainly candidates who have taken this route. Ron Paul's Campaign for Liberty, for example, is an organization that seeks to reform the Republican Party and spread the seeds of liberty throughout our public discourse. If you do decide to run as an outsider in one of the major parties, this book will still be very helpful, especially in your primary contest.

I formed *I CAN*, the *Independent Candidate Action Network* to help liberty-minded Independents and minor party candidates raise money, build coalitions, design and create campaign materials, hire campaign staff, and offer solid strategy advice.

This book is intended to build a solid foundation for anyone interested in running for elected office. The main focus of *18 Steps to Win A Local Election* is marketing, political strategy, and campaign management. **It is important that you do not rely on this book for legal advice**, especially for financial reporting and fundraising. **Legal requirements vary from state to state and precinct to precinct and this book is not intended to offer such counsel.** Check with your local lawyer and the Election Office before you begin your race.

There has never been a better time to be a candidate. **Go get 'em!**

18 Steps to Win a Local Election

⟋⟋⟍ Step 1: ⟋⟍⟍

Know My Compass

In this book, we'll speak of Independents as anyone who is not running as a mainstream Republican or Democrat. There are over 42 million registered American voters who consider themselves Independent. By minor party candidates, this book is referring primarily to the Libertarian, Constitution, and Green parties—the largest minor parties in America and around the world. There are also other minor parties that spring up from time to time, but they are usually personality-based and wither within a few years. There are also those who are working within a major party to reform it, like Ron Paul Republicans. This book is designed to help all these groups.

Since 42% of American voters no longer consider themselves affiliated with the Republicans and Democrats, you'd think there would be more information on how to win as an Independent candidate, but there isn't much in circulation. It turns out that Republicans and Democrats have been very successful in using fear to their advantage.

Most states strictly limit your ability to form a new political party or run for office under a minor party banner. These laws were created during the Red Scare of the early 20th century. Nowadays, politicians use the fear of terrorism, gay marriage, abortion, and social security to scare people into voting against "the other guy." This works. In the 2004 Presidential election exit survey, 25% of voters reported they were voting against the other candidate. They were voting out of fear.

Let's look at where the minor parties are in the United States at the beginning of this century. Most minor party activity was dealt a serious blow on September 11, 2001. As happens in times of national tragedies, most voters began to rally around the President, and financial contributions were diverted from politics to relief efforts. Many minor parties suffered great financial distress and the landscape changed enormously.

There is currently one national minor party, some regional minor parties, and multiple micro-parties. The Libertarian Party is now over 36 years old and has over 600 elected and appointed public officials in all 50 states. The Green Party is in second place with just over 200 public officials in 27 states. Both the Libertarian and Green parties have active international organizations around the world. The Libertarians have done well in Eastern Europe and Central America, where they are typically known as classical liberals. The Greens have done well in Western Europe and the Americas, most notably in Germany and Mexico. The Constitution Party claims to have the most registered voters and to be the third largest party in the U.S., but lags behind the Libertarians and Greens in elected officials. Other minor parties have come and gone in recent years but have few, if any, elected officials. There are also micro-parties. They often exist in just one city or state. The Charter Party is a very successful example in the city of Cincinnati.

The entire political culture in the United States is currently undergoing a rapid transformation. For many years, Libertarians and Greens ran mere skeletons of a party, and this is still true in many states. This means that there are Libertarian and Green party officials who have regular meetings and activities at the national and state-wide level, but their activity has only recently fleshed out into solid political progress on the ground. Former Speaker of the House Tip O'Neil is famous for saying, "all politics is local." This is where the Libertarian Party is doing better than ever before and will continue along the path of fleshing out the party. The Greens have active local groups on the East and West Coasts in the so-called "blue states" of the Democratic Party and in major metropolitan areas.

As the organization and financial strength of minor parties continues to improve, the mundane tasks of running a political party are now easier than ever before. The Internet has dramatically leveled the playing field in politics. Just a decade ago, sending out press releases, communicating with members, coordinating events, and doing political research was difficult, expensive, and time consuming. The digital revolution has enabled the growth of successful minor parties and Independent campaigns.

U.S. politics are also changing rapidly with technology. More people now identify themselves as Independents rather than Democrats or Republicans. Information is available to the American voter as never before and many are taking this opportunity to question their old beliefs and traditions. This is an excellent opportunity for a candidate to introduce themselves and their political party.

There are two reasons most people give for their Independent political status: They don't like the idea of political parties, or they don't believe in the philosophy of the Republicans or Democrats.

The number of Americans repulsed by political parties continues to rise. Most of this disgust comes from the corruption of the two major parties. A kind of mystique has been created. This aura is similar to that generated by big Hollywood movie stars and creates a false sense of invulnerability and inevitability. "Republicans and Democrats: your two choices in politics." It is important to remember that political parties are simply groups of people with similar ideas who work together to elect some of their members. Since most Americans are relatively unfamiliar with the activities of minor parties, it's difficult to know if new parties would change their outlook. If you find yourself in this category, you may decide to remain completely Independent and join a support group like *I CAN*.

If you simply dislike Republicans and Democrats, then perhaps you'd prefer to join a minor party. Many people think minor parties are all alike. The national news media does not take much time to explain the differences. Before you look at those other parties, it's helpful to examine your own beliefs. Unfortunately, most Americans learned in high school or college that the full spectrum of political thought could somehow be expressed in a line. This line originated with the seating arrangement of the legislative bodies during the French Revolution. Aristocrats sat on the right and commoners on the left.

◀━━▶

Communist   Democrat   Republican   Nazi

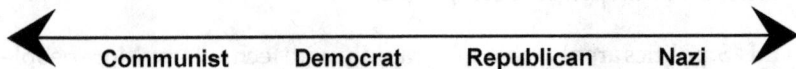

**If we think things through, this chart really doesn't make
a lot sense.** Most people in the media and in polls think that since
Independents are not conservative or liberal they must be "middle of
the road" or "moderate." But this line, and its simplistic assumptions,
ignores whole groups of people. It is especially easy to spot the flaws
when we mention real-life extremes. For example, where would
Thomas Jefferson and George Washington fit? How about Gandhi or
Queen Elizabeth I? An improvement to this line was created by David
Nolan and is called the "Nolan Chart."

**This Nolan Chart categorizes political leaders based on two
axes: economic liberty and personal liberty.** Ron Paul, Jesse Ventura,
Barack Obama, Michael Bloomberg, John McCain, and Hillary Clinton
have been scored based on their votes and public statements. You can
score yourself on the next page.

(Please note that Libertarian indicates a philosophy, not just the
political party by the same name.)

Step 1, Figure 2: Nolan Chart

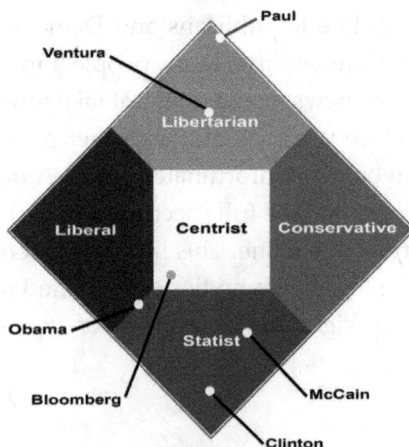

Answer the following questions and give yourself 20 points for every "yes," 10 points for every "maybe," and 0 points for every "no." Plot the personal and economic scores separately and see where they connect. For example, if I answer "yes" to every economic question, I would score 100 points. And if I answer "yes" to every personal question, I would get 100 points. The dot on the chart below shows where 100 meets 100 on the chart.

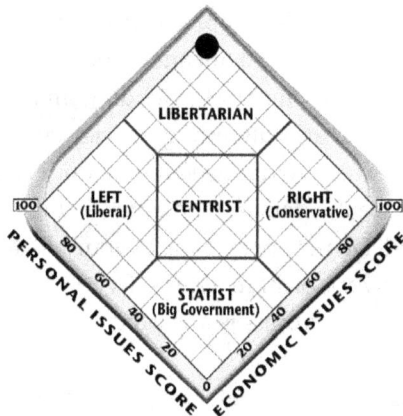

Personal Issues

1. Government should not censor speech, press, media or Internet.
2. Military service should be voluntary. There should be no draft.
3. There should be no laws regarding sex for consenting adults.
4. Repeal laws prohibiting adult possession and use of drugs.
5. There should be no National ID card.

Economic Issues

1. End "corporate welfare." No government handouts to business.
2. End government barriers to international free trade.
3. Let people control their own retirement; privatize Social Security.
4. Replace government welfare with private charity.
5. Cut taxes and government spending by 50% or more.

The Candidate

The candidate of a political campaign has a very specific job. Never forget that you must persuade a majority of the electorate to vote for you on Election Day. Sounds pretty basic, but most candidates who lose their races have not kept their eye on the ball. Let's examine that goal in more depth.

First, in order to persuade people, you must communicate with them. For most local races, that means knocking on thousands of doors, printing campaign materials, sending mail, speaking with the press, posting signs, and attending special events. This book is designed to explain exactly what needs to be done and how to do it. You, the candidate, are the person who must do most of these things. Do not get distracted. Do not spend time in your headquarters. Do not spend time on paperwork or in meetings. Every moment you are not communicating with your voters is a wasted moment.

Second, you must communicate with people who are persuadable. Do not waste time arguing with a person who has made up their mind. Your campaign is not a debate. You do not win if one person changes their mind or by shouting louder than everyone else. Always be polite. Agree to disagree and get away from people who have already decided as quickly as possible. Preaching to your choir is almost as bad as preaching to your opponent's choir. Thank your supporters, listen to their issues, and move on. Undecided voters are your target, you must spend most of your time and energy finding them and speaking with them.

Third, you must persuade the people who will actually vote on Election Day. Senior citizens, married people, homeowners, and wealthy people vote much more often than young, single, renters, and poor people. But placing these generalities aside for a moment, you must specifically identify the voters who are most likely to vote for you on Election Day and focus your efforts on them. This is called **Targeting,** and is described in Step 4 of this book.

There are several characteristics of successful candidates.

Confident. A successful candidate has the confidence of knowing he or she is the best person for the job and isn't afraid to explain why. A candidate may occasionally feel nervous, but he or she swallows that nervous energy and makes it work to his or her advantage. A successful candidate is never too confident or arrogant; underestimating your opponent and the difficulty of your task is deadly.

Authentic. Voters today crave authenticity. Speak from your heart about things that really matter. Don't preach or intellectualize your subject matter. You may have a great speech about "Live Free or Die!" but your constituents want to know that you care about their families and can fix the pothole on 12th Street.

Truthful. The best candidates are truthful, honest, and direct. As an Independent or other minor party candidate, you favor some ideas and are against others. Learn the best way to explain your position in a precise and direct manner, and never lie or invent statistics. Do not hem and haw on controversial topics. On the question of abortion for example, you are likely to lose half your audience whether you answer yes or no. But if you stumble through a complicated answer, you will lose your complete audience. They will assume you are uncomfortable with the subject and therefore untruthful. Most voters are unaccustomed to hearing Independent solutions to our public issues. Study and practice your explanations and answers so that they can come through clearly. If you do not know the answer to a question, fully admit your lack of knowledge. Write down the voter's contact information and get back to them as soon as possible with your answer.

Punctual. Good candidates are always on time or slightly early for their commitments. A candidate's time is their most precious commodity, but never even begin to think that your time is more valuable than your audience. When you arrive late, you've already broken your first promise. And we all know what voters think of candidates who break promises. Sometimes it is tempting to stay late at a particular event. Perhaps there's even a valid reason to do so, but this is why you have your staff. Your personal assistant's job is to interrupt you when necessary and keep you on schedule. Staff members can stay behind while you are whisked away to your next appointment.

Polite. All successful candidates are polite and civil. The easiest way to kill an angry voter is with kindness. Agree to disagree and move on. You will meet stupid people, obnoxious people, and painfully frustrating people, but they all vote. If you are polite, you will earn points with everyone you meet. It is especially important to be cordial and polite with your opponent. This can be difficult in a heated campaign, but never take your opponent's remarks personally. You're a professional candidate now, you must show your professionalism by answering your opponent in a manner suitable for public discourse. Never accuse your candidate of any behavior or respond to a personal attack without consulting your campaign staff. You must have concrete, irrefutable proof of any accusations against your opponent or your credibility will rapidly evaporate.

Well-groomed. Your public appearance must convey professionalism at all times. A good rule of thumb about clothing is to imagine what everyone else will be wearing and dress slightly better. If you plan to introduce new solutions to your community, you need all the help you can get. Your independence or association with a minor party has probably done some damage to your credibility already. If you do not appear to be completely professional, you will be easily written off as a kook.

Informed. When explaining your policies, you must be ready to cite local statistics and examples of how your vision will benefit the people of your district. This is especially true for Libertarians who may be explaining complicated concepts. Always use local examples to illustrate complicated ideas. Information works two ways. You must listen to the concerns of your voters and then cite those concerns in your examples. You will learn much more about your district from speaking with the voters than you ever could have known before. Be open to listen and learn.

As a minor party or Independent candidate, you must keep in mind that most voters either have no opinion or are misinformed about your party. Your constituent base may even include people who publicly exhibit psychological problems or anti-social behavior and are falsely labeled Libertarians, Greens, or Independents by themselves or the media. Your credibility may already be suffering from your association with a minor party. In order to counteract these problems, it is necessary for you to be ten times the candidate of your opponent. You must outshine, outwit, and outlast your opponent at every opportunity. You must be the most professional candidate your community has ever seen. In this way, you will dismiss the false rumors about your party and show your true colors. The more credible Independent candidates in your area, the smaller this problem will be.

In medium to large scale campaigns, most of the candidate's time is spent fundraising. You wouldn't know this from watching TV, but all major candidates like Barack Obama or John McCain spend most of their waking hours on the telephone raising money. For Independent candidates, this is even more important because you do not have a major party's deep pockets to tap. Find out how much money the candidates spent to run for this office the last time. You need to raise at least as much as they did to be competitive. If you raise more money, you can either outspend them or keep it for your next race.

Step 2:

Know My Political Organizations

The Libertarian Party

Libertarians believe that individual liberty and personal responsibility are two sides of the same coin. They also believe that government is the least efficient method of achieving public results, at best a necessary evil. Therefore, governments should only perform the absolutely necessary activities that no other organizations can, such as the legal system, law enforcement, and national defense. Libertarians are tolerant of others, even when they don't approve, and consider moral issues outside the scope of government. Many voters are confused by Libertarians' views. The LP can appear to be ultra-conservative on economic and property rights issues and ultra-liberal on social issues. In reality, Libertarians are neither right nor left. They trace their roots back to such notables as John Locke, Adam Smith, and Thomas Jefferson. They strongly defend all the rights listed in the Constitution and want to cut government spending and taxation by over fifty percent. Many Libertarians are spiritual and attend church just as regularly as the general population, but they do not consider laws governing morality to be productive or desirable.

The Libertarian Party has a national office in Washington D.C. and fifty-one state affiliate parties including the District of Columbia. There are over six hundred elected Libertarians in each of the fifty states. The national party is governed by the Libertarian National Committee whose officers and representatives are elected at a biannual national convention. State parties differ in their structures, but resemble the national party. Internationally, there are Libertarians active in over a hundred countries from Australia to Zimbabwe. Libertarians have been the most successful in Costa Rica, where they control ten percent of the national legislature, and in Eastern European countries where they are often known as "classical liberals."

The Green Party

The Green Party of the United States is a federation of state Green Parties committed to environmentalism, non-violence, social justice, and grassroots organizing. Whether the issue is universal health care, corporate globalization, alternative energy, election reform, or minimum wages for workers, Greens feel it is necessary to take on what they call "the powerful corporate interests." The Green Party has ten key values: direct democracy, social justice and equality, ecological wisdom, non-violence, decentralization of wealth and power, community-based economics, feminism and gender equity, diversity, personal and global responsibility, and sustainable development.

The Federal Elections Commission recognizes the Green Party of the United States as the official Green Party National Committee. They are partners with the European Federation of Green Parties and the Federation of Green Parties of the Americas. Internationally, the Greens have been most successful in Western European countries, especially Germany, where they have shared a leading role in parliament. The Green Party has also formed successful coalitions in Mexico.

The Green Party decision making body is the Coordinating Committee, composed of delegates from each accredited state party. The Green Party of the United States was formed in 2001 as a reincarnation of the older Association of State Green Parties (1996-2001). In 2008, the Green Party National Convention nominated Cynthia McKinney for the Green Presidential ticket. There are currently 220 elected Greens in office in 27 states.

The Constitution Party

In 1992, a coalition of independent state parties united to form the U.S. Taxpayer's Party. The U.S. Taxpayer's Party's goal was to limit the Federal Government to its constitutional boundaries and to restore civil government to the principles our country was founded upon. Some of the state affiliate parties have adopted the national party name, while others have adopted or retained a different name.

The Constitution Party champions the principles of government laid down by our founding fathers in the Declaration of Independence and the U.S. Constitution, principles which they feel have been abandoned by the political establishment. They expressly endorse the Christian faith, stating that Jesus is the "Creator, Preserver, and Ruler...of these United States."

The Constitution Party is pro-life, pro-gun, pro-American sovereignty and independence, and in favor of a strong national defense. It is also anti-globalist, anti-free trade, anti-deindustrialization, and anti-unchecked immigration. They also oppose special rights for homosexuals, the constantly increasing expansion of unlawful police laws, and both foreign aid and military interventionism.

The Constitution Party holds a national convention every four years to nominate a Presidential candidate and approve a platform. The National Committee is composed of representatives from the state affiliates. There has been some controversy within the party and several state affiliates have separated from the national party.

As you can see, the Libertarian, Green, and Constitution parties are quite different. The Libertarians focus on personal liberty, the Greens focus on equality, and the Constitutionalists focus on liberty within the context of Christian values. These are the three largest minor parties, but there are many others. You should investigate your options and then decide what's best for you and your campaign.

Independent Coalitions and Non-Profits

Whether you decide to run as an Independent, a minor party candidate, or a major party reformer, you must build your coalitions. There are plenty of politically active groups today, and many of them are strictly non-partisan for purposes of tax exemption or their legal status. As an Independent you must bring together some of these groups for your common cause. It will prove essential for fundraising, finding volunteers, and getting local endorsements.

Here is a list of groups that can help you and your campaign in a variety of ways.

The State Policy Network is the only group in the country dedicated solely to improving the practical effectiveness of independent, non-profit, market-oriented, state-based think tanks. They have local think tanks in nearly every state. http://spn.org

The Campaign for Liberty is Ron Paul's group dedicated to promoting and defending the great American principles of individual liberty, constitutional government, sound money, free markets, and a noninterventionist foreign policy, by means of educational and political activity. http://www.campaignforliberty.com/

The CATO Institute was founded in 1977 by Edward H. Crane to increase the understanding of public policies based on the principles of limited government, free markets, individual liberty, and peace. http://www.cato.org/

The National Center for Constitutional Studies is an educational organization founded by Cleon Skousen, famous for books: *5,000 Year Leap* and *Making of America*. http://www.xmission.com/~nccs/

The I CAN Independent Candidate Action Network is a peer-to-peer network of voters, volunteers, and candidates dedicated to promoting Independent and minor party campaigns.

The League of Women's Voters is a nonpartisan political organization that encourages informed and active participation in government through education and advocacy.

You must carefully study and participate in your local political landscape. Successful politicians move like ducks through water. Be sure you have yours in a row.

❧ Step 3: ❧

Prepare for Winning Office

As a potential candidate, your focus inevitably becomes winning. How do I win a campaign? How do I run a successful campaign? The electorate, however, is focused on why they should vote for you and your qualifications.

The voters are looking for a competent person to lead their community. While they may be pleased with your political philosophy and your campaign, you need to demonstrate preparedness to govern. Your professional and educational background is important. Most community colleges offer night courses in community development, urban planning, and government. Brush up your skills. Taking classes and perhaps working toward a degree in these fields will demonstrate your interest and ability as well as help you govern more effectively once you win.

Candidates also need to do thorough research on all local or state-wide issues that may come up during the campaign. Don't be surprised if voters want your educated opinion on an issue that has nothing to do with your office. Pick a quiet place in the library or in your home office to read voraciously any and all newspaper and magazine articles about politics in your area. During this time, it's an excellent idea to start your own reference book. Include your notes, photocopies of important articles, maps, or interesting stories in a three-ring binder. Memory is often imperfect, and you don't want to waste your time during the campaign trying to remember something you should have written down. If your opponent contradicts himself in public, it is extremely helpful to show reporters quotes from previous news articles at the very moment of the contradiction. Voters will inevitably ask you about an issue you know nothing about. When this happens, write down their name and contact information to call them back with your answer within the same week.

Developing a strong and vibrant public life is another essential ingredient a potential candidate needs to groom early. A public life refers to becoming active in your community at some level. There are many ways to become a community leader, but you should publicly pursue at least two or three activities you enjoy. If your goal is political, it is important to become active in your local minor party or issue-oriented community groups. Some local Libertarians or Greens are more interested in discussing problems than actually working on solutions. In this case, it is a good idea for you to lead a special sub-committee of people who really want to work for change. Your example may energize your group and bring in more active members.

There are also non-partisan political and social clubs in most cities. Their main goal is to advance a cause or provide a venue for political speakers. This kind of group is great for making contacts. You may wish to join a social service club such as Toastmasters, Rotary, Lions, or the Kiwanis. If you are religious, you may decide to become more active with your church. Perhaps you have a special hobby, interest, or sport. Your profession may have a special association or union. You can search for a group that suits your interests in the community calendar of your local newspaper, in the library, or on the Internet. Where a local club does not exist to support your interest, start one. A public life is necessary to demonstrate your ongoing commitment to your community, build contacts, and live a generally balanced life. Public service will promote your political career and bring innumerable benefits to your personal and professional life.

As you meet people and make contacts through your public and personal life, it is vitally important to keep a professional record of their information. You can purchase a one inch, three-ring binder in your favorite color from any office supply store. Inside your binder you will place a calendar insert. You will add alphabetical contact information inserts, and alphabetical plastic sleeves designed to hold standard business cards. Day Runner, Inc. makes excellent inserts for this purpose, but any brand is fine. You should create your own contact book because prepackaged agendas will include many items you don't really need, may not include enough space or pages, and will add to your clutter. Any time you meet a person for whatever reason, ask for a business card and be ready to produce one of your own. If they have a business card, that's great. Write a note to yourself on the card as to how you met, and tuck the card immediately into the alphabetical sleeves in your binder. If they do not have a card, ask them to fill out their contact information. Be sure to get email addresses; they will play a significant role in your campaign. Discretely obtain the person's birth date if possible or any details about their family and take notes.

While we are on the topic of public service, let's include a brief word about public speaking. Surveys have shown that public speaking is the number one fear of most Americans, ranking just higher than death. Public speaking is the first skill many candidates must learn. Everyone can benefit from improving their public speaking skills. Toastmasters International is a group specifically formed to practice speaking in public. Its members are very friendly to new guests. Membership is generally less than thirty dollars, but you are welcome to attend your first few meetings without being a member. You can find a local Toastmasters group on their website at http://www.toastmasters.org/, or in your newspaper's community calendar. Toastmasters makes public speaking more enjoyable with local, regional, national and even international competitions that help a member to improve in a fun and accepting environment. It is highly recommended that you join this group if you do not regularly speak to audiences of at least twenty to fifty people. This is the typical audience size for most local campaigns.

Now that you are developing a public life, you should consider the degree that you will mix public with private. People you don't know may now recognize you in the street, at church, or scooting through the supermarket. You need to keep this in mind. My rule when I manage campaigns is: private is private and public is public. Keep your home as your inner sanctum. That means your home address and phone number are unlisted and off limits. Your children are off-limits. Don't have publicized events in your home. Your office is public. Whenever you are outside, you must be dressed and groomed appropriately. No more quick runs to the corner store in boxers. When you were anonymous you might have pulled it off, but you're now becoming a public figure.

Your Financial Affairs

Prepare your business and financial affairs for public scrutiny and the disruption of a campaign. Whether you run your own business or work for someone else, your finances and those of your employer or partner will come under close examination by the media, the general public, and your opponent. Just the appearance of impropriety or conflict of interest could be disastrous for your campaign. Speak confidentially with your spouse, your business partners, and your accountant. Make sure that all of their taxes have been paid. Be sure that all your employees, including domestic help, are legally employed and that you have met all federal, state, and local requirements. If you have a business, it may be a good idea to hire an outsider to look things over and check for any irregularities your current accountant may have missed.

You may be able to manage a business or work full-time during the early phases of your campaign, but prepare to be a full-time candidate at least four months before your election to local office. (Note: If you are running for a relatively minor local office, the time constraints are proportional to the public's interest in the office. A position on the local land or water management board, for example, may only require your attendance at certain "meet the candidate" luncheons and dinners.) If you are employed, you should take your boss's temperature concerning your potential campaign. If you own a business, you need to plan for your absence. Just because you set your own hours does not mean you can continue to practice law, sell real estate, or run a business while you're campaigning.

Running a political campaign may be the most exciting adventure of your professional career, but it is also physically and mentally exhausting. A candidate must focus on winning. In a campaign, as in business, there is always something you could be doing to reach new voters. Planning to do both at the same time is a recipe for disaster. At some point after you make the final commitment to run, it may be a good idea to speak with your important clients about your upcoming political campaign. You may decide to assure them that there will be no disruption of service, outline your plan for maintaining your level of quality, and introduce them to any employees who may be assisting them in your absence.

Step 4:

Pick the Right Race
at the Right Time

Aim small, miss small. Mel Gibson gave this excellent piece of advice to his children in his famous epic movie *The Patriot.* It is wise to set reasonable goals and plan your line of attack. Look for the smallest public office you are qualified to serve in. This may even be an appointed position in a local committee. Many people are surprised to learn how much work is done by appointed committees of interested citizens. Many times, there are vacancies in these committees due to apathy. This is the perfect opportunity to get your feet wet in local politics without the expense and drama of running for office. It also demonstrates your ability to govern and willingness to help your community. Serving in an appointed position will increase your contact with the various interest groups and constituencies in your district.

Part of your research is attending the public meetings of the office you plan to seek. An enormous amount of information can be collected at these meetings. Pay particular attention to the work of any future opponents. Take detailed notes of each meeting and how you could perform more effectively. More often than not, you will quickly identify issues the public is unhappy with and the weaknesses of your possible opponents. It is important for you to outline your plan to improve local governance. And when you win, you certainly want to know how the meetings are conducted.

Local Elections Office

Pay a visit to your local Supervisor or Board of Elections and the Secretary of State's office. Both of these offices usually have handbooks and guidelines on all the rules, regulations, and deadlines a candidate must follow. First, take a look at their websites. Every year, these websites are getting larger and more complete. You may even be able to download handbooks on election law without leaving your house. Information varies from state to state and county to county, but you can often discover how much money your opponent spent on his campaign, who contributed to his campaign, and vote totals by precinct. This information will help you decide if you can successfully compete for a particular office. Please be careful with all the information you collect from these websites. They are not always up-to-date, and are often listed as "unofficial."

Elections workers generally know their job and their legal requirements very well. They are usually very helpful and friendly. Before you decide which office to run for, you should get their list of upcoming elections and the qualifications for each office. Typically, there is a residential requirement, deadlines for specific documents to be filed, possible petitions to complete, and other legal details.

It is a very good idea to hire an elections lawyer to occasionally advise you throughout the campaign. You may decide to have this lawyer keep track of your deadlines and requirements, but a very conscientious assistant could handle the same tasks. In most cases, local candidates will not need legal counsel aside from the beginning and ending of their campaigns.

You must always confirm deadlines and vital legal information with the often pleasant people who work in the local or state elections office. Some legal requirements may be so confusing that even lawyers disagree on what they mean. Be sure that you and your lawyer are operating on the same wavelength and have the same understanding of the law that these employees operate under. Always be friendly and never argue with an elections official; they can and will make your life difficult if they want to and possibly ruin your chances of winning office. (Of course, you can always sue them, but your case won't be resolved until after the election is over.) If you feel an elections worker is mistaken, simply get their advice in writing. Their interpretation may eventually be proven incorrect, but you have protected yourself if you have followed their written advice.

When speaking with elections workers, always be polite and cordial, but remember that you are better off not saying much. Do not state your intention to run or seem overly curious about any particular office until you are ready to make your public announcement. Assume that anything you say at the Election Office is in the public domain, and may be repeated in the press or privately circulated to your opponent.

Campaign Strategy

There are just three questions that will determine the course of your entire campaign. How many votes do I need to win? Who will vote for me? How can I get enough votes to win? This last question will be addressed in later chapters.

How Many?

The short answer is 50% plus one. First we need to determine how many citizens typically vote in the race you are running. Pay a visit to your local Elections Office website. You're looking for how many people voted the last time this office was up for election. Add the totals of the candidates and divide this number in half. This is the number of votes you would have needed the last time. Now check the previous cycle's election numbers for this office. If the two numbers are relatively similar, split the difference. You now know how many votes you will probably need to win. As you will see in these examples, winning office depends as much on when you run as where and how.

Example 1. Off-year elections.

John Smith ran against Joe Jones for Plymouth Township Trustee in 2003. Smith won 3,285 votes to Jones' 1,324 votes. The total number of votes is 4,609. So the minimum necessary to win the trustee race in

2003 was 2,305 votes. In 1999, Smith ran against Larry White. Smith won 3,112 votes compared to White's 1,738. In 1999, the winner needed 2,426 votes. This gives us a fair idea that a candidate needs roughly 2,400 citizens of Plymouth Township to support him on Election Day. Let's round that number up to 2,500 to play it safe.

Step 4, Figure 1: Example 1, Off-year Elections

Votes	2003	1999
Larry White		1,738
John Smith	3,285	3,112
Joe Jones	1,324	
Total	4,609	4,850
Needed to Win	2,305	2,426

Example 2. Even-year elections.

In Ohio, the Presidential election was in 2000, and the Governor's election was 2002. The Plymouth Township Planning Commission election is held on even years. In this case, we need to consider whether it's a Presidential year and if there are any special factors in the race. In 2000, 12,000 citizens cast their ballot for the Township Planning race. In 2002, only 8,000 voters came to the polls. In 2004, the most contentious Presidential race in Ohio's history, a full 16,000 voters came to cast their ballot. So on Presidential years, you may need as much as 8,001 votes. In Gubernatorial years you may need only 4,001 votes.

In Example 1, there was little difference between running for office in an off-year or the next. But in Example 2, the differences were quite large, in some cases doubling from one election year to the next. In Plymouth Township, it appears quite obvious that an Independent would have a much better chance winning the Township Trustee race. The two major parties get their constituents so excited on the even years that the Planning Commission looks like a long shot, especially during Presidential years. If you are interested in winning, it is very important to consider these timing factors. When calculating how many votes you need to win, be sure to include at least the last two election cycles similar to yours.

Who?

Now that you have determined how many votes you need, you need to ask, "Who will vote for me?" Looking at a map, we might ask, "Where will my votes come from?"

Let's imagine that you live in a perfectly square-shaped district with three very distinct neighborhoods. Cherrybrush Estates is the wealthiest part of your district. You went to Americanfactfinder.com, and you discovered that the average income was $90,000 per capita. The average age was 50, and 45% of the residents have college degrees. Oakview is the middle class neighborhood where the per capita income is $50,000, the average age is 35, and 30% of the residents are college educated. Pinewood is on the wrong side of the tracks, with mostly apartments and low-income housing. The per capita income is $25,000, average age is 25, and only 10% of the residents have graduated college. Let's look at the election results from these neighborhoods in your district.

Step 4, Figure 2: Timing Example

	Cherrybrush	Oakview	Pinewood	Total
Averages				
Income	90K	50K	25K	
Age	50	35	25	
College Degree	45%	30%	10%	
Registered Voters	5,000	8,000	7,000	20,000
Republican Votes	2,500	2,000	500	5,000
Democrat Votes	1,000	2,000	2,000	5,000
Independent Votes	500	1,000	500	2,000
Total Votes	4,000	5,000	3,000	12,000

The scenario in Figure 2 illustrates a great example of how an Independent can win if they run against only one opponent, but not against two.

It also shows that registered voters who do not vote can make a big difference. Educated and wealthy voters are much more likely to vote, and thus have a greater impact on the election. This is why it is so vitally important to pick the right race at the right time. You can practice picking real life examples in the *18 Steps to Win a Local Election Workbook*.

Step 5:

Speak with My Priority Contacts

There comes a time in your planning when you must decide to commit yourself to running for a particular office. Before you make this decision, it is important to speak with the leadership of your political party or Independent coalitions. Make an appointment for a quiet conversation with your city, county, or state chair in a private office or at home.

Be prepared to present your case. You should offer evidence for why you are the best person to run for the office you are seeking, how you will be able to afford your absence from work, and how you plan to raise money for your campaign. Your party chairman or executive director will want to be assured that you are serious about seeking office before he or she decides to help or endorse you. You should consult with the party leadership and be open to their suggestions about which office you should run for. As a candidate, you need to remember that you are a part of a team of candidates running for office. Your interests must coincide with the interests of your party if you expect their assistance in raising money and locating volunteers.

When meeting with your party leadership, be clear about what you bring to the table and what your needs are. You will need campaign staff, volunteers, and money. The leaders of your party can help you identify a campaign manager with experience, a list of potential volunteers, and a list of financial contributors. Don't be surprised if you need to purchase the list of contributors; it is the party's most valuable asset. If another party member is seeking the same office, the party is obligated to treat you both fairly and equally.

Now make a list of everyone you know. They could be family, friends, mentors, business contacts, political contacts, or acquaintances from your church or social club. Divide this list into four parts according to their level of importance in the community and their emotional closeness to you.

Your most important contacts should include just five people. Arrange time to speak with each person privately. Consult with them before you decide to run for office and before you decide which office to pursue. The rest of your list should be divided accordingly: 20 to 30 "VIP's," 100 to 200 "Priority Contacts," and then the rest are considered "General Contacts." You should discuss the "vague possibility" of running for office with your VIP's including especially your wife, grown children, and close family friends. Their reactions will speak volumes. Listen to them. We will use the other three portions of your contact list later in this book. The biggest mistake a new candidate can make is running for the wrong office at the wrong time without support.

Now you are finally ready to make a decision to campaign and for which office. Announce this decision to your immediate family, friends, and your party leadership. Be clear that this is an informal announcement with a public one soon to follow. Take your spouse out to dinner and celebrate. Now is the time to return to your list of contacts and start dialing. Make appointments to meet with all your VIP's to make your informal announcement in person. Your VIP's should be treated like the important people they are. Inform them that they are the first to get the news of your big decision. Make them feel like an integral part of your effort. At this time, you can informally create your campaign committee.

Offer your VIP's a special place on your strategic planning committee and invite them to regular meetings. They may or may not decide to become active in your campaign, but they will be very flattered that you asked.

You want to speak with as many of your contacts as possible before making your public announcement. People like to feel they are a part of something special and are joining your effort at the ground floor. Everyone treasures secret knowledge. Make the most of this private preparation period to include everyone you know on "the secret." This can be a valuable time for fundraising. You will need "seed money" to get things started.

While preparing for office, it is vitally important to have the support of your immediate circle of family and friends. It is no coincidence that so many of our political leaders are divorced. The demands of a campaign are nearly continuous. A typical campaign involves long hours away from home and exhausting work. Relationships are bound to suffer. Be clear with your family about what a campaign costs in terms of your time and energy. Plan ahead to have special time set aside for your spouse and children before, during, and after the campaign. Plan now for a vacation after the campaign is finished. During the difficulties of the campaign, remind yourself and your family of that special time you will have together after it's all over.

By this time, you have notified all your contacts that you are planning to run for office. A whisper campaign may already be starting on your behalf. You may now begin to float the official trial balloons. You've probably heard this expression used before by journalists. Essentially, you will begin to tell large groups of people in your public life that you plan to run for office and which offices you "have under consideration."

It is especially important to speak with any business groups you are a part of and your church group or social club. These groups are usually fairly representative of your constituent base and their reaction will give you a good idea of how the general public will accept your announcement. You should receive a polite if not warm reception to the idea of your running for office.

There's generally at least one gloomy Gus per ten people in the room, so don't let one objection or apparent apathy get you down. If there's a substantial amount of rejection among your public acquaintances, be careful; it may be the first sign of trouble. Try to find a good opportunity to pull an acquaintance aside and probe for reasons why your group was hostile. You may find out they're just hungry, or there may be serious obstacles to your campaign. Either way, you should not take rejection personally. Thank people for their honesty.

❧ Step 6: ❧

Appoint My
Campaign Committee

"A camel is a horse designed by committee."

- Sir Alec Issigonis

You may now publicly start your official campaign committee. Requirements for campaign committees vary; be sure to comply with your local laws. Most election offices require at least a chair and a treasurer, while some require more. In most states, the treasurer is legally responsible for following all campaign finance laws and filing the related documentation by certain deadlines. Your treasurer must have a strong background in bookkeeping and be a very responsible person. Even minor financial mistakes can lead to large fines, a media scandal, and possible jail time. Your treasurer should study the financial reporting requirements very closely and include the deadlines in your overall campaign timeline.

Always check over paperwork and deadlines with you local elections officials. Sometimes deadlines are incorrectly posted or written in a confusing manner. Once you have a treasurer and follow your local requirements, you need to open a bank account in the name of your committee. Since September 11th and the USA PATRIOT Act, banks have become stricter about starting campaign accounts. You may need to obtain a tax payer ID for the committee or be willing to use your own Social Security number. Thankfully, it is quite simple to request a taxpayer ID (known as an EIN or Employer Identification

Number) online at the IRS website. You do not need employees or to pay income tax to qualify. Campaign committees are recognized as not for profit.

Your Campaign Committee can be honorific or a real working committee. The choice is yours, but it is essential that the candidate be ultimately responsible for anything done in his or her name. You can be advised by this committee, but they exist to support and to serve, not to dictate strategy or campaign plans. There will be certain legal requirements that must be filled according to your state or municipality. The treasurer is usually the only person with real legal liabilities, but this varies. The real work of any campaign is usually conducted by the paid staff or volunteers at the direction of the campaign manager. The Campaign Committee can be somewhat in charge of strategy, but it is mostly a mechanism for raising money and letting your VIP's feel they are a part of the campaign.

Chair. The chair of your committee is essentially the public leader of your campaign. This person should be a respected figure in the community and in the local government if possible. In large campaigns, there are often several co-chairs. The position is largely ceremonial, and it is often offered to the largest financial contributor to the campaign.

Vice-chair. The vice-chair of your campaign is in charge of meetings when the chair is not present. This is another ceremonial position you should save for an influential person.

Secretary. The secretary is responsible for taking the official notes of the meetings, reading the minutes of the previous meeting, and distributing agendas. If your campaign committee is purely ceremonial, the campaign staff may decide to complete the secretary's official duties.

Treasurer. The treasurer is responsible for collecting all the fundraising income and campaign expense data and properly reporting this information in the correct format and before the appropriate deadlines. This person must be very responsible and detail-oriented. An accountant or bookkeeper is perfect but not necessary. Most campaign finance forms are easier or similar in difficulty to filing personal income tax forms such as a 1040.

Finance chair. The finance chair is the lead fundraiser for the campaign. The ideal candidate has some successful fundraising experience, or is a successful business or sales person. Try to find someone with a well-established list of wealthy connections that does not overlap your own list.

Candidates may decide to have other staff positions participate in the campaign committee. Libertarians and other minor parties have a tendency to give a great deal of importance to committee work. It is absolutely essential that the campaign committee play a purely advisory and support role. The candidate, the campaign manager, and their consultants call the shots in any successful campaign, not the committee. Do not allow yourself to be absorbed in committee work. Every moment you do not spend communicating with an undecided voter is a minute you have wasted.

Step 6, Figure 1: Sample Campaign Committee

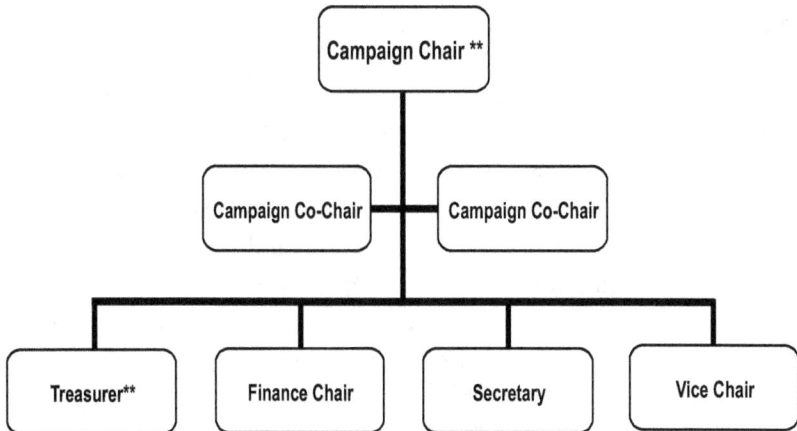

** Often the only legally required positions. Check with the local Election Office.

Step 7:

Hire My Campaign Staff

You will now need to locate and hire a campaign staff. There are essentially ten roles your campaign must fill with either hired help or volunteers. Most local campaigns will not be raising or spending enough money to hire paid staff. In this case, any money you do have for staff should be spent first on a good campaign manager. Other roles include: treasurer, finance director, scheduler, personal assistant, volunteer coordinator, strategic consultant, communications director, office manager, and field director. Some of these roles may be divided further depending on the size and scope of the campaign. In most local races, three or four people may share these roles. In micro-campaigns, one person may assist the candidate in all these roles.

Once you have decided upon a campaign manager, both of you should proceed to look for a suitable campaign office. Most micro-campaigns are managed from a candidate's place of business or home. This may be the only financially attainable space, but it is far from ideal. A local campaign of any size should try to find a separate office. Keep your campaign life as separate as possible from home and work. Many times, a personal or professional contact may have a location you can borrow for a few months. Try to find the least expensive accommodations that suit your purpose. An office needs to be reasonably secure with sturdy locks and an alarm.

Remember, this will be the headquarters for your campaign. It should be kept as clean and neat as possible, but does not need to be very fancy. There needs to be a large empty space for your volunteers to feel comfortable and for storage of your campaign literature and signs. Include as many tables and chairs as possible for your volunteers to work comfortably. You will need at least one private room for your campaign manager and treasurer to work quietly when they need to. This room can also be used for private strategy meetings and other business you may wish to conduct in private. Volunteers should be kept separate from paid staff and from your fundraising, accounting, and financial management. These matters require the confidentiality of a private office.

Discuss any additional needs with your campaign manager before you decide on an office. Communication is the single most important purpose of a political campaign. Investigate the costs and availability of the communications resources in your potential office space. One key aspect that is often overlooked is the availability of cable. Most cable companies now offer television, telephone, and broadband Internet services in one package. As of this writing in 2008, this will probably be the cheapest way to do all three things.

If you do not use cable television, is there high quality reception? Your staff will need a television in the office to stay on top of local news as it breaks and to record your appearances for future reference. Keep in mind that you will need multiple phone lines for voice, Internet, and fax. If you are planning a volunteer or paid phone bank, you may need many phone lines. A professional campaign will eventually need multiple computers with Internet access, a digital camera, a fax machine, a scanner, a photocopier, a paper cutter, staplers, file cabinets, shelving, cork bulletin boards, white boards, desks, telephones, trash cans, and a podium. Every item you do not have in the office will eventually be needed and turned into an errand. Plan ahead. Volunteers eat and use the restroom. Does the office have running water or quality restrooms nearby? Will you need to schedule delivery of drinking water? Keep these infrastructure needs in mind while selecting an office.

At some point, hopefully in your new office, you and your campaign manger will sit down and develop a campaign plan. Campaign plans include a message, fundraising, at least three budgets, a staff organizational chart, a timeline, and strategic details of how many votes you need to win and where to find them. Many aspects of the campaign plan are discussed in the following chapters but need to be finalized before you go public. Dwight D. Eisenhower once said that plans are useless but planning is indispensable. Remember that a political campaign is tremendously fluid and constantly changing. Your plans need to adapt to change. Don't feel trapped by them.

Step 7, Figure 1: Sample Campaign Staff

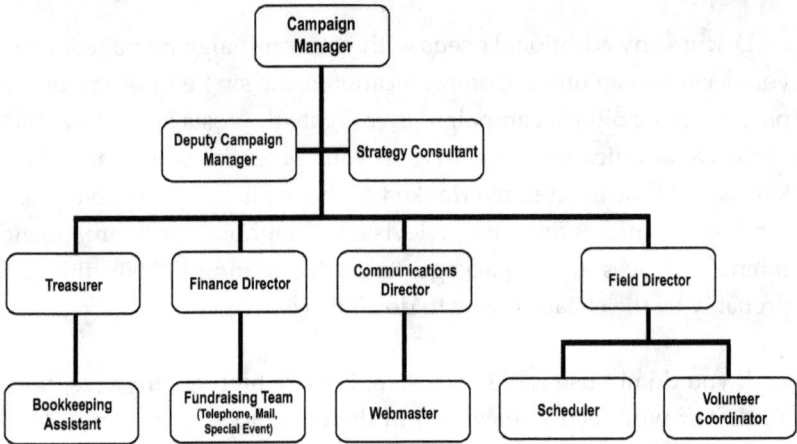

```
                        ┌─────────────┐
                        │  Campaign   │
                        │   Manager   │
                        └─────────────┘

    ┌──────────────┐              ┌──────────────┐
    │Deputy Campaign│─────────────│  Strategy    │
    │   Manager    │              │ Consultant   │
    └──────────────┘              └──────────────┘

┌──────────┐  ┌──────────────┐  ┌──────────────┐   ┌──────────────┐
│ Treasurer│  │   Finance    │  │Communications│   │    Field     │
│          │  │   Director   │  │   Director   │   │   Director   │
└──────────┘  └──────────────┘  └──────────────┘   └──────────────┘

┌──────────┐  ┌──────────────┐  ┌──────────┐  ┌──────────┐  ┌──────────────┐
│Bookkeeping│  │Fundraising Team│ │ Webmaster│  │ Scheduler│  │  Volunteer   │
│ Assistant│  │(Telephone, Mail,│ │          │  │          │  │ Coordinator  │
│          │  │ Special Event) │  │          │  │          │  │              │
└──────────┘  └──────────────┘  └──────────┘  └──────────┘  └──────────────┘
```

Campaign Manager

A campaign manager has the most difficult and time consuming task of the campaign besides that of the candidate. In small campaigns, the manager will fill most if not all of the roles of your staff and must be willing to work nearly endless hours. A manager must have the complete confidence of his candidate. The candidate will often need to rely on the manager for objective opinions on how well he or she is performing and for advice on how to improve.

There are essentially three types of campaign managers: professionals who travel from place to place in search of campaigns, part-time managers who are usually rooted in one geographic area but have other work in the off-season, and amateurs who help friends or fellow party members. Each type has its own strengths and weaknesses.

Generally, a professional campaign manager knows exactly how to win political campaigns and can be an excellent resource for first-time candidates. When judging a professional campaign manager, remember that most managers have what some people would consider a "losing" record. For example, if three Democrats and three Republicans run for their party's nomination, that's six different campaign managers and candidates running for the same office. If the Democrat wins the nomination, but loses the general election, it is still considered as a loss. A professional manager may often be stuck with a less than perfect candidate or do an excellent job in a very difficult, but losing race. Adding insult to injury, former candidates often blame their managers for losing. When interviewing a potential manager, it is much more important that they know what they are doing, show confidence, and be accessible, rather than have a good win-loss record. It is essential that you both get along with each other and work well together.

The weakness of an out-of-state professional is that he or she may not be able to adapt to your region. He or she may not have any established contacts with the community or have a feel for the kind of people who live there. He or she may be unfamiliar with the local issues. Some of your volunteers may even feel jilted that you hired a relative stranger and resent taking his or her marching orders.

The phrase "part-time managers" refers to individuals who may work part of the year in a different profession. This is especially common in Florida and other states that have elections only in even numbered years. This is a difficult kind of existence, as you may imagine. These folks often want to be full-time professional managers, but they are unwilling to travel in search of available campaigns in other states. Occasionally, these types of managers must continue to run their other business while managing your campaign.

There are benefits to this type of manager. They know the area they work in very well, and have many established political contacts. They know the local media well and may even have personal relationships with them. They usually have lists of volunteers and contributors to help in your campaign. Their fees are usually less expensive than full-time managers.

The weaknesses include: possible schedule conflicts between your campaign and their other business, less varied experience than the full-time professional, and baggage from previous races. Be wary of local campaign managers who have a reputation for burning bridges. Any negatives attached to your local manager may eventually be associated with you as well.

The third type of campaign manager is an amateur who may be a personal friend or a local party activist. This is probably the most common type of campaign manager in a minor party and this is one of the principal reasons minor parties have not established a more winning record. Be wary of those with little or no experience but behave as if they were crack political operatives. An amateur campaign manager must first be willing to admit he doesn't know exactly what he's doing but is willing to learn. The strengths of this type of manager include his fresh approach, personal friendship, and willingness to work for little or no money.

The weaknesses of an amateur manager are so vast that you must have an old political hand or professional consultant you can rely on to advise you for your key strategic decisions. Remember, with an amateur, you are both learning together. In minor parties, it is very common to find amateurs who feel they are professionals because they have participated in previous campaigns. A professional, by definition, has either studied political management (not political science) in a university or graduate school and/or has many years of paid working experience in both winning and losing campaigns.

Don't be impressed by anyone who has not received more than twenty percent of the vote in a minor party race as a candidate or a manager. They either chose the wrong race to run or were not serious about winning. Both are fatal mistakes to your campaign. Remember, you are not running to prove a point; you are running to win. If your campaign loses, your ideas have also lost. Be sure your campaign manager understands that. It is recommended that you lend this book to your amateur campaign manager and inform your professional or part-time manager that you've read this book.

Treasurer

The treasurer holds the most legal responsibility in your campaign in most parts of the country. (Please consult your local laws.) There are several ways to handle the legal liabilities often associated with the treasurer. In most cases, it is an excellent idea to have the treasurer perform the actual duties legally demanded. These duties include keeping a record of all income and expenses, filing all financial documents required by the government on time, and maintaining the campaign committee's compliance with the applicable finance laws. Sometimes, the treasurer will hire an accountant to perform these duties and simply sign the needed forms. Sometimes, in small campaigns, the campaign manager will perform these duties and have the treasurer sign the forms. This depends upon the situation and background of the treasurer, and his or her comfort level in signing documents that bring legal liabilities. In many states, the Secretary of State provides free or low-cost seminars for campaign treasurers. Take advantage of this opportunity. Ultimately, the candidate and the campaign manager must be absolutely sure that all of the campaign's legal requirements are met.

Finance Director

The finance director is in charge of fundraising for the campaign. Ideally, this person has a successful history in sales, real estate, banking, personal finance, or previous experience in political fundraising. The finance director is not afraid to twist arms, place hundreds of phone calls, plan events, and write letters in order to raise money for your campaign. It is a good idea for the finance director and the treasurer to be two separate people. Putting this person in charge of incoming checks and the treasurer in charge of outgoing checks helps ensure accountability. The outgoing personality needed for raising money often conflicts with the introverted type of personality needed to maintain the books. Watch for tension between these two, but it's usually a very good, well-managed tension to have.

A treasurer must be the most responsible and trustworthy person you know who is good at filling out forms and balancing numbers. Your finance director should be the friendliest, most successful salesperson you know, and don't be afraid to sweeten the pot with a commission for funds raised.

Communications Director

Your communications position has very specific requirements. Look for someone with a background in public relations, advertising, news, marketing, education, or the printing industry. Your communications person must have an excellent command of the written and spoken word, be relatively attractive (if appearing on TV), and have some media contacts.

A media consultant is typically an outsider you hire for occasional help, while a communications director works on your staff. In a local campaign, it is usually not necessary to hire a full-time communications person as your manager will likely be taking calls from the media. But if you can find a volunteer who is an especially good writer or a friend who works in or teaches journalism, ask this person to help you write press releases, organize press conferences, and create your campaign materials.

In small campaigns, you may be issuing press releases and communicating with the media anywhere from once a month to once a day, but it is important to do so professionally.

Field Director

The field director is in charge of your ground game, including all your campaign events, door-to-door activity, getting out the vote, and roadside sign placement. The ideal field director likes to be on the road meeting volunteers and planning events with the scheduler.

Scheduler

Your scheduler keeps track of the campaign calendar. Your scheduler will take the fall for canceling appearances or saying no. This person must be detail-oriented, patient, and charming. It is very important to have only one official campaign calendar and only one person who can approve commitments. Start your campaign calendar by going to the local office supply store and buying a three-ring binder of the scheduler's favorite color, month and day-at-a-glance calendar inserts, alphabetical contact inserts, and a package of colored pens. There are also many great web-based calendars out there, like Google Calendar, that allow everyone on your staff to view your calendar from their computer. It is still good to have a paper back-up.

Begin the calendar by filling in the mandatory filing dates required by law and of course the Election Day itself. After filling in specific legal deadlines, count at least three days before them to place reminders. For example, "Note to scheduler and campaign manager: Remind Sally that she must file our Finance Report before Thursday." You don't want to think about filling out forms on the day they are actually due. Next, fill in any known appointments including space for family time and days off. You will use this calendar when creating your strategic campaign plan, setting times for scheduled mail drops and other media buys, as well as for noting appointments and other events. Your scheduler should create a color code to indicate the importance of a particular event. This will help the scheduler in his juggling act.

Time is the most valuable asset of your campaign. The scheduler and the campaign manager need to work together very closely to ensure that the candidate's schedule is full and that the events, appearances, or appointments are worth the candidate's time. In local campaigns, plan for your candidate to knock on every voter's front door. In most cases, this is not possible, so you will need to prioritize. Nevertheless, it is essential for your candidate to spend all of his or her time communicating with the public. Unless speaking with a reporter, time spent in the headquarters is entirely wasted.

Buddhists often talk about the importance of empty space. The empty space inside of a glass makes it useful for drinking. The empty space inside a house permits you to live within it. The candidate has simple human needs which must be met and accounted for within the schedule. This may sound obvious, but many candidates go without lunch or dinner because their scheduler forgot to place it between their appointments. The scheduler needs to be absolutely positive that there are empty spaces in the schedule for traveling times and possible delays. There must also be a break between being outdoors and indoors. After all, a candidate needs a shower after knocking on three hundred doors on a summer day. If a candidate is on the road, the scheduler needs to be sure the candidate has a place to eat and sleep, as well as freshen up between events.

As a candidate, don't be surprised if voters approach you with all kinds of requests for your time. Any appointment or request for a candidate's appearance should be referred to the scheduler. Politely take down all the relevant information, along with a contact number, and promise that the scheduler will call back with a confirmation. If you know that you can't make it, or feel the event would be a waste of time, inform the person that there may be a conflict, but you'll pass it along to your scheduler in any case. Place the burden of saying no on your scheduler. Remember candidates are the ones who choose to run for election. Don't blame your scheduler for making you busy; that's their job.

Your scheduler and campaign manager ought to be creative in the events they plan for you. It is their job to make sure that your time is used in the most effective manner possible. Any time you are not speaking with an undecided voter is a wasted opportunity. When you are not scheduled for events, you need to be out in the neighborhoods going door-to-door. Remember that you need time off as well. Unless you are under religious restrictions, choose a day off in the middle of the week. Saturday and Sunday will probably be spent at events or going door-to-door. You should be meeting each night with your campaign manager and scheduler to be sure you are up to date and know exactly what is expected of you the next day. Failure to do so will result in bumpy mornings, wasted time, missed opportunities, and hurt feelings.

Your Computer Team

There are actually a number of campaign functions that need competent computer volunteers. Among these are: webmaster, database manager, graphics designer, and social networker.

The webmaster may be a paid consultant or talented volunteer(s) who manages your website. Step 13 explains some of the best practices involving websites. The most common mistake among webmasters is that they design sites that appeal only to other webmasters or computer people. It is vital to the campaign that your web person or team is able to respond quickly to constantly changing situations and can create a site that is easy for the general public to navigate.

Your website is an integral part of your marketing material. It is important that the webmaster can work well with your communications director and can transform your printed material, audio-visual material, and data into a unified campaign message. It is no small task.

Your webmaster will also be in charge of sending mass emails to your voters, volunteers, and financial contributors. Be sure to find someone who is experienced in sending mass emails.

The voter database manager is a specialty part-time position that requires a good working knowledge of spreadsheets and database programs. The work involved is relatively simple for those familiar with these types of programs. It is recommended you find a techie volunteer who has a few hours per week to help out. The Elections Office can provide you with a list of registered voters and their contact information. The data is often available in a variety of formats. Most elections officials are very cooperative in this regard. Your techie volunteer can help you decide which format is best.

There are several decisions you will need to make regarding your overall strategy, but we can go through several of the most common lists your database manager will generate. You will need a mailing list, a walking list, a phone list, a volunteer list, and a fundraising list.

The mailing list is culled from the voter registration data. This is the list you will use for mailing promotional materials. Your budget will determine how many and what kinds of voters you include in your list. Since different lists in each state include different kinds of data, you may need to adapt these guidelines.

First, you want to separate everyone who voted in the last general elections and primaries. If your budget allows it, include people who voted in the last four to six years. Don't go back more than six years. If someone has not voted in six years, it is highly unlikely they will vote in your election or even live at the same address.

After you separate by date, you want to sort by party affiliation or which primary they vote in. Libertarians, Independents, and other minor parties are usually a relatively small portion, but be sure to make them a priority. These voters need to know who you are. Also be on the lookout for voters who change parties to vote in open primary states. These are swing voters who may be open to your message. You also may decide to develop different messages for the different parties. For example, you may wish to send a message critical of your Republican opponent's lack of economic responsibility to people with Republican voting records, and criticize the lack of social tolerance and civil liberties to Democrats. (See Step 12.) This can be used even in three way campaigns since your mailed material is specifically targeted.

The walking list will be used by you and your volunteers when campaigning door-to-door. There are special programs that place houses in a logical walking order, but you can easily do this yourself by sorting registered voters by street address. The walking list should be limited to people who have voted in the last six years. These voters will need to be printed on labels and stuck on index cards or sheets of paper. Labels of people living at the same address should be stuck to the same card. Include as much legible information as possible on the labels. You must include: names, addresses, phone numbers, party affiliation, and precinct number. Include the precinct name and voting location if possible. (See step 16.)

The phone list should be sorted similar to the mailing list and according to your strategy. If you have plenty of phone volunteers, feel free to go back more than six years but always make recent voters a priority. Print your phone list in an easily legible way for your volunteers. Sometimes spreadsheets can be very difficult to read.

Your volunteer and fundraising lists will be created by the campaign. It is a good idea to speak with previous Independent candidates as well as your local and state parties to gather contact information about people interested in volunteering or making financial contributions. Your treasurer and finance director need to work together to keep accurate records in a database for easy reference. Be sure your volunteer coordinator keeps good records on volunteers and their hours.

Remember that many states and municipalities require "in kind" donations to be reported. When someone donates physical items to the campaign, this is often called an "in kind" contribution. For example, if a volunteer offers to make t-shirts with his computer, the materials he uses are given to the campaign (i.e. the shirts, the iron-on labels, and the ink). This may be considered an "in kind" contribution if he purchased the supplies with his own money. Be sure to check the laws of your community as they may vary. The volunteer coordinator must keep track of these contributions and report them to the treasurer in a timely manner. Many states only require reporting when cumulative contributions reach a certain level within a certain time. As people may contribute money and "in kind" contributions over time, you must keep an accurate list of who does what and when.

The graphics designer is ideally someone you know with a background in advertising and marketing who knows how to use graphic design software. Ask to see some examples of their work. The designer needs to work together with the communications director and the webmaster to produce a unified brand and "look" for the campaign. Campaign letterhead, brochures, fliers, yard signs, and website should all have this same "look." This is called branding. Branding is very important. Just as you can spot a Coca-cola bottle from across the supermarket, voters need to be able to spot your yard sign among the forest of signs along the highway.

Social networking has recently become the number one activity on the Internet. As of this printing, websites such as Facebook, Meetup, LinkedIn, and MySpace have become new ways for people to meet and organize their social and professional lives. New social networks are popping up everyday and are becoming more specialized. Some social networks focus on one topic such as music, religion, race, or location. Your ideal social networking volunteer is someone who keeps up with all the latest trends in this field and already has lots of social network connections they can share with you.

Volunteer Coordinator

Think of the friendliest motivated person you know who has some management experience and a little free time they can contribute to your campaign. Convince this person to coordinate your volunteer effort. The key to volunteer coordination at the local level is friendliness and motivation. Find a responsible person you have trouble saying no to.

Most people who support your campaign are willing and able to volunteer in some capacity. It is important to match up their willingness and ability with the proper function. There are several general categories most volunteers fall under.

Party Hosts. Some people love to host parties in their home. This is an excellent opportunity for you to meet voters. You may even be able to recruit more volunteers and raise money. If anyone offers to host a campaign party, there are certain things you can do to make this party more successful. Scout the house out in advance and be sure it's suitable for your purpose. Create an invitation flier to mail to your host's friends, family, and neighbors. Be sure that everyone within a half mile gets that flier, including businesses!

Door-to-Door. Outgoing outdoors people should help you with your door-to-door campaign. Practice with these volunteers so that they know how to fill out the voter information cards. (See Step 16.) Explain the importance of filling out the voter cards correctly and sticking to those talking points. Be sure that they know your campaign message and stay on that topic with the voters.

Door-to-door volunteers should never fabricate or embellish answers to voters' questions, especially if they are unsure of the candidate's position. They should call over their coordinator or the candidate to answer voters' concerns right away. If that is not possible, make a note for the campaign to call that house with an appropriate response as soon as possible.

Office Volunteers. Office volunteers come in to the campaign headquarters and perform a variety of tasks. They may serve as receptionists and secretaries. They may be the campaign scheduler. They may read the daily newspapers and clip any stories of potential interest to the campaign or spot possible events for the candidate. It is important to have at least one competent person in the office at all times. Be sure that one person is responsible for receiving the mail each day and distributing that mail to the proper person.

Phone Volunteers. Some people are more comfortable than others making phone calls to people they do not know. Phone volunteers can call undecided voters, invite people to campaign events, give targeted messages to specific demographic groups, and conduct get out the vote operations. A crucial factor for phone volunteers is proper motivation. Whether they are working from home, or preferably in the headquarters, phone people need to work together in groups to stay on track and motivated. If you give someone a list to go home with alone, you can never really be sure that the work is getting done. Even very well-intentioned volunteers quickly get distracted or de-motivated when they are home alone.

Extras. Extras are happy to come to events, but don't want to do much else. These people are actually more important than you may think. You need to generate excitement and energy at your campaign events. Empty rooms do not help this cause. Extras are volunteers who can help your news conferences, your fundraising dinners, and your victory party to be that much more successful. They may even help defray your costs.

Be sure that the volunteers are actually able to perform the task they want and/or are assigned to do. It's rather common for well-meaning volunteers to bite off more than they can chew. A good coordinator checks regularly on volunteers to be sure the work is completed correctly, helps when needed, and tactfully reassigns volunteers in trouble. The coordinator must make sure each person is a good match for their task and feels useful to the campaign.

Step 8:

Identify My Spending Priorities

Perhaps the most important decision in any campaign is to set spending priorities. Call together your top advisors and staff and go over the financial records of previous candidates for your office. It can be very instructive to see where money has been spent in the past. This can also be an excellent guide as to how much money you need to raise to be competitive.

Looking at previous reports for candidates of the same office, you can estimate your budget for this year's race. We are going to create three budgets: a worse case scenario, a competitive scenario, and a best case scenario.

In the worst case scenario, we are going to take the average money previous winning candidates have spent in this race in the last three cycles and cut it in half. We will set up your spending priorities as if you had half the money it would normally take to win.

In the competitive scenario, we are going to use the average money of previous winning candidates and add fifteen percent. We are adding the money to account for undocumented help the previous candidates probably received from their parties. Then we will set up a new list of spending priorities based on this amount.

In our best case scenario, we are setting a stretch goal. If we collect double the money previous candidates have needed to win, what will our spending priorities be?

Now, here is a common problem with many small campaigns with Independent candidates: you raise a lot of money up front from your immediate friends and family, but the money starts to fall short near the end of a campaign. So, it is vital that you spend the money on your top priorities first, even if they are events far into the future.

For example, candidate Rogers calculates that his worst case scenario is to raise $5,000. He and his staff decide that if they are only going to raise $5,000, they better spend that money on a website and sending three postcards to all their voters in the three weeks before the election. In May, they start campaigning and actually raise $5,000 pretty quickly among Rogers' friends and family. So they buy a web domain, find a volunteer webmaster, purchase a bulk mail permit, go to a photo studio, then design and print all the postcards they might need.

In a second example, candidate Smith also calculates his worst case scenario as $5,000. He easily raises the first $5,000 among his family and friends. In fact, it was so easy that he decides to hire a fundraising consultant to do even more fundraising. Together, they spend $1,000 on the consultant and $2,000 on a fundraising dinner for all his co-workers and some party activists. He is an unknown minor party candidate, so he loses money on the expensive dinner. It turns out that his consultant has only worked for major party candidates. Now he doesn't even have enough money for his postcards or radio commercials. He has also alienated some of his original contributors and party activists for mismanaging his campaign money.

Meanwhile, candidate Rogers raised $5,000 in May. He spent almost all the money on his website and his mailing scheduled for October. When he visits community outreach events, he hands out extras of the postcards so people will remember him. As the months go on, he slowly raises another $5,000. He's now competitive. He orders 3,000 yard signs, and his volunteers spread them throughout the community. He keeps making phone calls and visiting people. His friends decide to have a fundraising party in their home, serving cheese and crackers. An artist he knows paints small portraits at the fundraising party. Some other friends are musicians and accept donations to serenade the guests. In the last few weeks of the campaign, he has raised more than anyone expected, and now he's running commercials on the local talk radio program and expands his mailing.

Since Rogers consulted his advisors and planned his priorities well in advance, he didn't have to make difficult spending decisions during the busy and tiring days of the campaign. He also had set goals for himself that encouraged him to continue raising money even after he was competitive.

Candidate Rogers set his priorities:	
First $5000	1. Website 2. Post cards for 3 mailings
Second $5000	3. 3,000 yard signs
Anything over $10,000	4. AM Radio ads 5. More mailings 6. Billboard on highway

Candidate Rogers is simply an example. Your campaign may decide on different priorities, but it is essential that the candidate and the campaign manager understand and agree on these crucial priorities in the earliest stages of the campaign.

Step 9:

Create My Budget

After you have set your priorities, creating a budget becomes much easier. We set our priorities based on low, medium, and high expectations for our fundraising success. Continue this process and create three budgets for weak, competitive, and strong campaigns. The *18 Steps to Win a Local Election Workbook* provides a detailed template for creating your three budgets in one spreadsheet.

Begin your budget process by looking over the financial expense reports of other candidates for this office. This gives you some ball park ideas of how much items cost and where you may want to spend your campaign money. You also have the benefit of 20/20 hindsight to determine which expenses were effective and which expenses weren't necessary.

While working on your budget, you will need to investigate the true costs of your office, your phone service, your mileage, bulk mail permits, website hosting, etc. Make the budget as detailed and as accurate as possible. Take time with your staff and try to calculate every conceivable cost. In fact, ask all your top staff members to create their own three budgets and bring them to your budget meeting.

A Sample Competitive Budget (Local Campaign- for 4 months)	
Advertising	
Postcards	$5000
Bulk Mail Permit	$180
Postage	$500
Business Cards	$100
Refrigerator Magnets	$200
Radio Ads ($15 x 10 ads x 10 days)	$1500
Office	
Office expenses (phone, Internet, supplies)	$400
Rent	$1000
Photocopies	$100
Travel	
Gasoline	$1500
Rented Convertible for Parade	$150
Parking Fees	$50
Total	$10,680

This may be your competitive campaign budget. What would you cut back? What would you buy first? What would you add if you raise more money? What if you can borrow a free office? These are the questions you should answer before the race begins.

Step 10:

Plan My Fundraising Income

There are many, many ways to raise money and your campaign should be as creative as possible. Here's a list of the most common ways, but don't let this list limit your creativity. Do make sure and check the laws in your state, especially if you plan any type of gambling, bingo, or raffles. They may be illegal.

Remember that you need to open your campaign with your local elections office and get a bank account *before* raising or spending any money on your campaign.

Put the *Fun* in *Fun*draising

Do you remember the ultimate peer pressure game in high school or college called *Quarters*? If a person bounced a quarter into a cup, they could make another player to do something he/she wouldn't ordinarily do. It usually involved romance and/or alcohol. Another popular game was *Truth or Dare*. The object of these games was to have fun pushing people outside of their normal comfort zone. You need to do that with your campaign fundraising. That's why games of chance are often so popular (and often illegal, so consult a lawyer). Make your fundraising plan fun for your contributors!

Pledge Cards

Before you ask for any money, your campaign needs a professional-looking pledge card that brings to life the "look" and message of your campaign. Made on cardstock, they should be easy to photocopy in color or black. They need blank spaces for all the data required by the Elections Office, credit card info, and your campaign address in case it's being mailed.

Family and Friends

Before your campaign publicly begins, you should ask your friends and family members to each meet with you privately. Be prepared to persuade them of the benefits of your campaign, why you are running, and be clear about how they can help. Show them your budget plans and how much money you need to raise to be competitive. Ask for volunteer time in addition to money.

Telephone and Mailing Lists

Obtain as many telephone and mailing lists as you can from clubs, churches, and other organizations you are affiliated with in your area. Focus most of your efforts on like-minded political groups such as your minor party or local association, political action committee, or non-profit organization. Some of these groups can give you lists for free, some may charge you, and some may not be permitted.

In most local races, the candidate must make the bulk of the phone calls, but the Finance Director should also be calling. Follow up telephone conversations with a prompt letter, return envelope, and pledge card. Thank the contributor for their pledge.

Most local campaigns will not have a budget for bulk fundraising mailers. If you do, target your local political activists and minor party members. Do not randomly send letters to your potential voters to solicit money.

Website

Your website definitely needs a contributions page. Make sure that you collect all the data you need for your reporting requirements. There are numerous methods for capturing this information. Please be sure to do it in a secure manner to protect both the campaign and the contributor.

Like all fundraising, your website contributions page needs to be creative. In 2003, the Howard Dean campaign had a bat that would become red as a new goal was being met. The red bat soon became a prop at Dean's rallies. All of his online donors were "in on the secret" of why he carried a red bat. Try to turn fundraising into a game.

Another creative fundraising tool is the online web store. There are many turnkey online stores like Cafepress who will manufacture and distribute all the items in your store. You just upload your logo, select your products, and let the company do everything else. They typically send checks once per quarter.

Fundraising Events

Typical fundraising events are dinner or cocktail parties, outdoor barbecues, and chili cook-offs. Breakfasts are popular since pancakes are inexpensive. Chili cook-offs ask for people to compete which is nice because they cook all their own food. Sometimes people schedule morning coffees or after-hours events.

The crucial aspect of a fundraising event at the local level is that it must not cost the campaign much money. In fact, you should find people who are willing to host the event and pay for the food themselves whenever possible. That's why local fundraising events often happen in people's homes. The candidate should never have a fundraiser in his own home. It can be a lose-lose proposition. If the candidate's home is too nice, people might think twice about your fundraising need. If your home is too shabby, people might think you aren't a good enough candidate.

When planning a fundraising event, plan little opportunities where people can spend additional money. For example, during your next fundraiser, hire an artist to come and draw sketches of your guests. Hold a silent auction. Or hold a real auction if you know a great smooth talker to be your auctioneer. Be creative. The idea here is to persuade your guests to spend a little more than they were originally planning.

Ask your guests for money at least three times during your fundraising event. The first ask might be the admission fee. The second ask is the silent auction. The third ask might be a campaign progress report from the manager. The fourth ask could be the candidate making a personal appeal. Be sure to remind your contributors how much work the candidate and the volunteers have accomplished with so few dollars, and how much more remains to be done.

Thank your contributors. Everyone who volunteers and contributes to the campaign should get a thank you note. Local campaigns are usually small enough that each person should also get a personal phone call from the candidate as well.

Plan Your Fundraising

Just as you plan your expenses, you need to plan your income from fundraising. Calculate how much money you will need for the entire campaign and how much you will need to raise each day, each week, and each month to achieve that goal.

Don't stop fundraising just because you have met your goal. If you have raised more than you expected quicker than you expected, just keep going. Plan another party. Make more phone calls. When people send you a contribution, they have a vested interest in your campaign. Don't be shy about asking them to contribute more at a later date. Invite all your past contributors to your fundraising parties. You can either spend more money on advertising, or you can save it for your next run for office. Nothing impresses and discourages future opponents like the size of your campaign war chest.

Rogers' Fundraising Sources Plan (Sample)	
1. Friends and Family (personal visits)	$3500
2. Business Associates (personal visits)	$1000
3. Minor Party members (phone calls)	$3000
4. Barbecue Fundraiser at Bill's House	$1600
5. Cocktail Party at John and Linda's	$1600
Total Plan	$10,700

After you win office, continue to hold fundraising parties at least once every six months. You want to build up your reserves for a possible run at an even higher office some day, or just to make the next campaign a little less frantic.

After you win office, you should assemble a special newsletter or collection of your press clippings for your contributors. Show them what a great investment they made in your campaign. Keep your campaign account open so you can pay for these items, and never use government employees or equipment for campaign purposes.

Step 11:

Control My Expenses

There are several methods to ensure financial accountability in your campaign. Before implementing any of these methods, make sure they are permitted in your area. First, have one person responsible for depositing money, and a second person responsible for writing checks. You can require two signatures on all checks. You can place an expiration date on your checks such as "Not Valid After 30 Days." Always avoid cash transactions, and always have a witness when cash is being counted. Have the witness sign a cash report recording the figures. You can require your campaign manager to sign each monthly bank statement to verify that he received and reviewed it. Be sure that your treasurer has the proper software to manage the deluge of information. Always make photocopies of checks before they are deposited and keep them on file.

It is vital that the top staff: candidate, campaign manager, and the treasurer, understand the campaign expense reporting requirements for your race. Every expense must be accounted for with a receipt. If someone spends money on the campaign and cannot produce a receipt, congratulate and thank them for their contribution, but do not reimburse them.

Your staff should meet once per week to discuss campaign expenses, where you are in fundraising, and how much cash is on hand. The budget should be compared to actual expenses and adjusted. Checks can be signed, bills paid, and invoices reviewed at this meeting. Reaffirm your priorities in light of fundraising results. Discuss the ups and downs of the previous week and set goals for the next week.

Always, always remember that properly controlling your expenses and sticking to your plans is just as important as the fundraising itself. Just as Benjamin Franklin once said, a campaign penny saved, is a campaign penny earned.

Step 12:

Be the Answer
by Framing the Question

Your campaign message is ideally a narrative, a story about why you are the best person to run for this office. Joe Trippi once told me that a candidate is the answer to a question first framed by the campaign. The message will blend aspects of your biography, your philosophy, and your goals with the needs and desires of the public. Your campaign message, or theme, will determine whether you win or lose in the eyes of the public. Even if you do not hire a single staffer, you need professional help to develop your message. Ideally, your campaign manager or media consultant will do extensive research on how to target the voters you need to win and advise you in crafting a message. Even if you are running a micro-campaign, this is the one aspect on which you should consult with a political professional.

The winning candidate has the most compelling story told to the most voters. You are a unique individual with very specific experiences and characteristics that make you a special candidate for public office. The job of your campaign is to frame a question in the public's mind. The candidate's job is to be the answer to that question. So when designing a campaign message and a theme, it's a bit like the popular game show *Jeopardy!*. We know the answer is you, but we need to properly frame the question.

The Answer:

Barack Obama is a famous example of a candidate who is the answer for a specific question. In 2006, he was brand new to Washington politics and the national scene. He appears youthful and energetic. He plays basketball and has a young family. His speeches are hopeful and optimistic. He's the very first truly viable African-American candidate for President. Barack Obama is the change candidate. **His answer is: Change.**

The Question:

Who brings change to Washington? This is truly the only question Barack Obama answers. He is completely inexperienced. He doesn't have deep roots in his community. He doesn't have a background in executive management, foreign affairs, the economy, or the military.

In this example, we see that the candidate's story is the campaign, and the campaign centers on the question Who brings change? So the timing of the race is very relevant. If Obama had been running for President in 1984, no one was voting for change in the good times. If Obama had been running in 2004, most people were still too afraid of 9/11 to vote for change. So not only was Obama the answer to his campaign's question, he was also the answer to his election cycle timing: everything's wrong, and we need something new.

While crafting your story, it can be helpful to compare and contrast yourself with your opponents. Look at the chart on the next page. This is called the Candidate Grid. This grid can help you frame any campaign to help you plan your message and map out your opponent's possible responses. You need to do this at the beginning of your campaign. But it also needs to be constantly updated and re-examined after you have read your opponents' campaign literature or listened to them speak. New information may necessitate a change in your message grid, but you do not change it lightly or often. You need to balance the need to be consistent with the constantly changing situation of the campaign or the community. (Obama was constantly under pressure to change his message, but he never did.)

Candidate Grid

McCain on **McCain**	1. War hero 2. Strong, stable 3. Experienced 4. Maverick, willing to vote against party and self-interests 5. Puts his country and the common good first.
Obama on **McCain**	1. Warmonger who has been damaged by war 2. Hot-tempered 3. Stuck in the past 4. Erratic, unpredictable 5. A good man at heart who is "out of touch" with reality
McCain on **Obama**	1. No military experience 2. Weak, unstable 3. Inexperienced 4. Chicago party machine 5. Votes according to popular opinion polls and to please radical elements of his party
Obama on **Obama**	1. Community Leader 2. Strong, Innovative 3. Brings Change 4. Fought his party his entire career 5. A new kind of leader for America's new century

Your Issues

After you have determined what question you answer, you can fit issues into your message. There are likely to be at least two or three burning issues in your community. In the case of micro-campaigns like the planning or water commission, you may need to create your own issues to enliven the campaign.

First, people must know that you care. Then, they want to know what you care about. Always remember to frame your campaign in a positive manner about the positive impact you can have in your community.

In the preparation phase of your campaign, you should be attending the public meetings of those you seek to replace. You should also be reading the local news. Look at all your notes. In most local races, it will become obvious what the key issues are. It's also a good idea to speak with your family, friends, and neighbors to find out what issues they have. As you go door-to-door, and as your campaign heats up, you may find that you've missed an important issue. Be flexible about altering or changing your message, just don't do it very often. More than once in your campaign, and you may wash out your message or appear erratic.

Two Meats and One Potato

Many candidates fall into the trap of addressing too many issues in their campaigns. Remember that you only have a limited amount of time, money, and volunteers. You can't address every issue. If you are having trouble deciding which issues to address, remember this good rule of thumb: two meats and one potato. That is, two solid, hard-hitting economic or property issues, and one soft human interest issue.

Partisan Messages in Partisan Races

There are several varieties of partisan races an Independent can expect to encounter. The three most likely categories are two-way (Republican vs. Independent or Democrat vs. Independent) and three-way (Republican vs. Democrat vs. Independent). Four-way races are uncommon but will be discussed.

The following strategies are recommendations on how to build your base of support while attacking that of your opponents. You must also build your own name identification and give voters a reason to vote *for* you, not just *against* someone else. John Kerry in 2004 made an excellent case for George Bush's incompetence, but he did not succeed in convincing voters that he was the right man to replace Bush. You must do both: convince the electorate that you are right person for the job, and that your opponent is not the right person. This is especially true if you are running against an incumbent.

Republican vs. Independent

The Republican vs. Independent race is very common in the Midwest, exurbia, and rural communities. The point is that these races are most likely to occur in regions of the country that are more conservative than average. The key to winning these types of races in conservative havens is to appear even more fiscally responsible than the so-called party of small government. You need to emphasize that you want an even smaller and less intrusive government that respects gun and property rights.

When thinking about and explaining your strategy and message, draw a line like this:

Step 12, Figure 2: Republican vs. Independent Spectrum

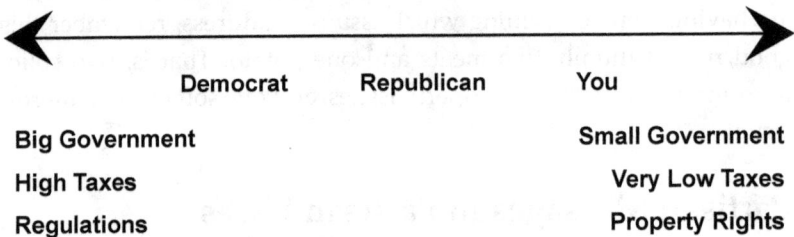

Democrat	Republican	You
Big Government		Small Government
High Taxes		Very Low Taxes
Regulations		Property Rights

This line will instantly clear up your message with conservative voters. They will understand that Republicans aren't as "conservative" as you are when it comes to issues they care about like taxes, spending, and property and gun rights.

Where Republicans are a governing party in many states as well as nationally, they have increased spending even faster than the Democrats before them. Find examples of local Republicans (and maybe even your opponent) raising taxes, heavily borrowing, and spending.

Most voters understand what "living on a credit card" is all about. It means that someone is spending more money than they earn and living in debt. Republicans across the country are "living on a credit card." They borrow money so they can increase spending without raising taxes. Do not confuse voters with bonds and other financial instruments. In a recent survey, a majority of voters confused owning bonds with owing bonds. (Of course, it's good to own a few bonds, a valuable investment.) They thought bonds were a government asset, not a liability. Simplify your language, "Democrats tax and spend, Republicans borrow and spend, Independents want to cut BOTH taxing and spending so government can live on a budget." Simplify these complicated issues with clear, common language anyone can understand.

There will usually be at least a small enclave of Democrats who live in conservative districts. Democrats can often be counted on to vote for an Independent instead of a Republican. Target Democrats for very specific phone calls and possibly a mailing. Remind them that you are the only non-Republican alternative in the race. Hit them with a message that will resonate with their issues.

Democrat vs. Independent

Democrat vs. Independent races are very common in big city urban environments, especially on the East and West coasts or in rural areas that still vote for old-fashioned Democrats. If you are fighting an old fashion Democrat in a rural area, use the same strategy as Republican vs. Independent. In big city urban areas, your race is most likely to be more liberal than average. The key to winning liberal strongholds is to emphasize your support for civil liberties, gay rights and marriage, and drug re-legalization. Portray your Democratic opponent as less committed to these ideas than you are.

Step 12, Figure 3: Democrat vs. Independent Spectrum

| | You | Democrat | Republican |

Civil Rights and Liberties   **Strong Military**

No Gov. Regulation of Marriage   **Regulation of Marriage**

Drug Legalization   **Drug Prohibition**

Jail for Violent Offenders

This the same line used in Republican races, but instead of focusing on conservative issues, we are talking about the issues liberal voters are concerned about. Most liberals have the misinformed impression that all liberty-minded Independents are ultra-conservative. This is obviously not the case on these issues: civil liberties, gay marriage, and drug legalization. Most liberals feel disappointed in their Democrats. Nationally, Democrats have been forced to "move to the center." This is actually a misnomer. They aren't moving to the center as much as they are trying to appear more conservative on cultural issues.

If you are an Independent running in a liberal community, your main goal should be criticizing the Democrats for running away from the above issues. Most Democrats voted for the Patriot Act and against gay marriage. Try to tie these issues into local politics and find local examples of Democrats ignoring civil rights and liberties. The gay community provides an excellent fundraising resource. They are also well organized for volunteer efforts. They could become your most important ally in an urban race if you make the effort to recruit them.

There will probably be a small number of Republicans who live in your district. Be sure to target them for specific phone calls and possibly a mailing. Emphasize the fact that you are small business friendly and the only non-Democrat alternative.

Republican vs. Democrat vs. Independent

The issues listed above under two-party races are called **wedge issues.** An ideal wedge issue divides your opponent's base of support while solidifying your own base. In three-way races, it is exceedingly difficult to hit both Democrats and Republicans with successful wedges. What you need in a case like this is called a **double wedge issue**. Emphasize the negative issues both Democrats and Republicans have in common. Focus on the "sameness" of the two parties, and attack their unfair monopoly on political power.

Some elections will have a run-off if no candidate receives more than 50%. If this is true in your race, it is more important for you to focus on choosing your opponent for the run-off. These races can get very complicated, but as a general rule of thumb, you should decide who you prefer to have as your opponent in the run-off and attack the other candidate to knock him out. That means that if you live in a conservative area and a Republican is ahead in the polls, you should begin focusing on him as if he were your only opponent. If you can succeed in knocking the Republican out, you have an excellent chance to win the run-off. If the Democrat falls out of the race, you have already worked on establishing your fiscally conservative message against the Republican. It's a win-win. The opposite would be true in a liberal district.

Another strategy in a three-way race is to allow your opponents to beat each other up while you travel the high road. Campaign on your strengths, not your opponents' weaknesses. While on the high road, remember that you must convince the voters that the incumbent does need to be replaced, and that you have the qualifications to do a better job.

Occasionally, you may find yourself in a four-way race or even more. In such a race, you must differentiate yourself from your minor party or Independent competitor. Never forget who your main competition is. Focus on your major party rivals. It is unlikely that your Independent competitor is as prepared or as serious as you are.

The Geography of Politics

Your specific race will undoubtedly have its own truly unique characteristics. Keeping this fact in mind, there are several broad categories of campaigns where you may find yourself. This section details which issues and messages have traction in particular geographic areas and constituencies. You need to tailor your message for your audience. This does not imply dishonesty or disrespect for your principles. It means quite explicitly that different people have different interests and reasons to vote. As a candidate, you must correctly identify and address the issues affecting your constituents, or you will never have, nor deserve, electoral success.

Geography and Demography

Geography impacts politics as it does all human activity. The politics of geography is rapidly changing in the United States as America becomes the fastest decentralizing civilization in history. This book addresses the impact of demography and geography beginning with the urban downtown and working outward. It is important to note the definitions used in this book as they may be different from common usage.

Urban Downtown City Centers

The urban downtown is the twisted reflection of an industrial bygone era. From the late 19th century through the 20th, industrial cities spread unevenly throughout the country. These cities were often strategically clustered near natural resources such as farm land, water, coal, and iron. Other cities grew due to their location as key distribution points. As people grew wealthier, they left the urban downtown and created the first suburbs. Many urban areas fell into decay during the 1970's and 80's. Many then rebounded with a minor explosion of art, culture, and entertainment in the 90's. Some cities fared better than others, some are less divided than others, but there are clear facts any Independent must consider when running for office in an urban downtown.

To be clear, this category is meant to include the city center with populations in excess of 350,000 within the city limits. These are roughly the 50 largest cities of the U.S. Some of these are: New York, Baltimore, Washington, Indianapolis, Columbus, Cleveland, Chicago, and Los Angeles. Other urban areas may be large when their suburbs are included, but this is not the definition used here.

The politics of these urban downtowns are usually dominated by Democrats and African Americans. Indeed, a county level map of the United States shows that Al Gore and John Kerry carried these urban downtowns exclusively even though they lost their elections as a whole. Democrats do so well in this environment that even politicians who smoke crack on national television with prostitutes can become mayors, and militant Islamists with wives walking three steps behind them can become councilmen. There is no question that both Libertarians and Republicans perform poorly in these areas. Greens do have success in the upscale areas of downtown, but continue to perform poorly in African American neighborhoods.

Until Libertarians and other minor parties can build urban party machines to rival their Democrat opponents and appeal more strongly to African Americans, campaigns in America's largest cities are often wasted efforts. The fact that Republicans nearly always run a paper candidate in these areas is yet another factor weakening prospective Libertarians or Constitutionalists. In a two-way race, an Independent could hope to attract some Republican voters, but two-way races are very uncommon in most large cities. In yet another quirk of geography, Republicans from downtowns are often social liberals, and attract much of a Libertarian's base of support.

Step 4, Figure 4: Median Income in Indianapolis – This map clearly demonstrates the classic rings surrounding a renewed downtown.

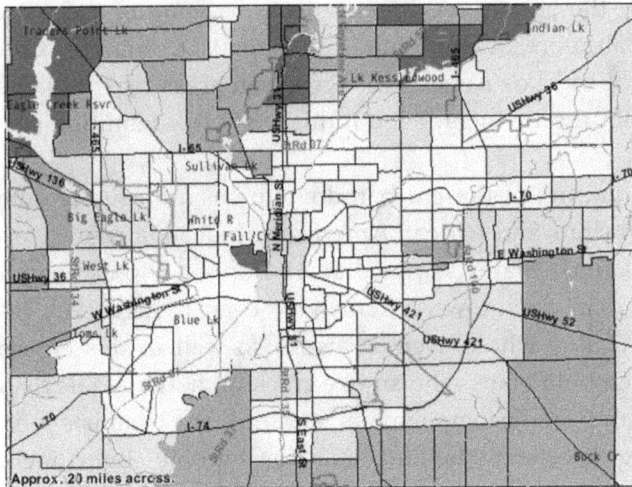

That being said, there are some promising developments that a downtown minor party can build upon. First, there is a blossoming revival of art and entertainment in many of America's downtowns. Political quiz results from downtowns show a strong Liberal-Libertarian leaning. There are several issues Greens and Liberal-Libertarians can build upon: gay rights and marriage, the war in Iraq, voter fraud, civil liberties, the war on drugs, and privacy issues.

John Kerry, in his effort to win the popular vote, alienated many of his fellow big city Democrats on these issues. It is also crucial for big city Independents to attract African Americans into their campaigns. Churches are often the key to African American votes in large cities. If Independents can convert some of these ministers and clergy, or at least be invited to speak at their services, this would be a large step forward. Some candidates find this mixing of religion and politics distasteful, but many cultures see them as natural partners.

A big city campaign will require many volunteers and full-time employees. Among your full-time staff, it is essential to hire a campaign manager, a fundraiser, and a communications director. A full-time volunteer coordinator is also necessary, but may be a volunteer. This book does not really include how to run in downtown urban areas, as these typically do not qualify as small local campaigns.

The Two Rings of Suburbs

Suburbs are now acknowledged to have formed double and triple rings around most cities. Often, there is a downtown area surrounded by industrial plants and ringed by the first suburbs. The first ring of suburbs was usually built between the early 1900's and 1950. In some cases, these first rings are already being torn down and renovated. With the effects of urban decay, it may be difficult to differentiate where the downtown ends and the first suburbs begin. This suburb is usually a racial mix of working class families and urban poor. Some cities have succeeded in rehabilitating these neighborhoods into hot, chic real estate markets for the artistic community. Other cities have let these neighborhoods degenerate into criminal havens. Either way, the politics in these communities are still typically controlled by Democrats and have many of the same negatives for minor parties, except for the Greens.

This initial ring is often enveloped by old office space, the first shopping malls, and light industry. This space divides the first and second rings of suburbs. The second suburban ring is often more conservative and a bit wealthier than the first (sometimes shockingly so). This ring is often segmented, and may include both Democrat and Republican neighborhoods. The politics of each particular neighborhood cannot be predicted by this book, as they differ widely even within the same city. A general rule of thumb, however, is that the Republican Party machine is alive and well in the second ring, and actively engaged with the Democrats.

When Republicans run for big-city mayor, they often live in the second ring where they have a strong base of support. Republican big-city councilmen are usually elected from the same second ring. The difficulty for Libertarians, Greens, and Independents living within the second ring lies in the weakness of their parties and branding. Many residents of the second ring would vote for a minor party if they had the opportunity to fully understand its philosophy and issues, but the active fighting between the Republicans and Democrats obscures the subtlety of Libertarianism and other minor party philosophies. These will almost always be actively contested three-way races.

Libertarians and Constitutionalists can win in the second ring of suburban neighborhoods through carefully orchestrated party building. It is vital for those in the second ring to build networks of volunteers, activists, financial contributors, and potential candidates. Getting out the vote and placing volunteers at every precinct are a must. Door-to-door campaigning and neighborhood evening parties are very important. A party machine must be built to effectively rival the ability of Republicans and Democrats to turn out the vote. In some cases, the Republicans and Democrats of a big city urban area will decide in advance that they will not compete in certain neighborhoods in order to save time and money. If you, as an Independent, can identify which offices and neighborhoods will not be three-party races, it would obviously be a tremendous advantage to do so.

Exurbs

Between the suburbs and the farms, there's a brave new form of community growing in the eyes of demographers and politicians these days: exurbia. Exurbs are geographically large communities with no specific center sprawled between cities in recently developed farmland or wilderness. Some exurbs are built around and take the name of old rural towns, but the new population shares nothing in common with the old. These communities are built upon the information age. Employment in the exurbs is focused around consumer services, hi-tech light industry, and web-based business. Their decentralization grew naturally from our ability to work wherever we could plug into the Internet. Exurbs are remarkable, yet slippery to define. They include new office parks, shopping centers, and new housing developments next to farmland.

In a recent column in the New York Times, author David Brooks explains:

> Ninety percent of the office space built in America in the 1990's was built in suburbia, usually in low office parks along the interstates. Now you have a tribe of people who not only don't work in cities, they don't commute to cities or go to the movies in cities or have any contact with urban life. You have these huge, sprawling communities

with no center....In my book I tried to describe the culture in these places – the office parks, the big-box malls, the travel teams and the immigrant enclaves. But when it came to marketing the book, I failed in two important ways. I couldn't figure out how to tell the people in exurbia that I had written a book about them. Here I was writing about places like Loudoun County, Va., and Polk County, Fla., but my book tour took me to places like downtown Philadelphia, downtown Seattle and the Upper West Side. The places I was writing about are so new, and civic life is as yet so spare, there are few lecture series or big libraries to host author talks. The normal publishing infrastructure is missing.

The very newness and lack of civic life mentioned by David Brooks is a huge comparative advantage for minor parties and Independents. Since Democrats and Republicans have yet to build party machines in these communities, Independents have had a lot of success in running for office. In fact, most elected Libertarians, for example, either live in exurbs or very nearby. This is not a coincidence.

Research done in exurbs indicates that the populations are highly mobile, well-educated, and Independent voters. Most exurbanites share very strong libertarian ideas. It is already well-known within the Libertarian Party that they are very popular with those who work in the information sector, and this is where they live. They believe that government is inefficient, corruptible, and largely unnecessary. Many of them moved from the cities to avoid the big city's crime, decay, congestion, and high taxes. They are very opposed to raising taxes in their new communities. Although Independent, most residents in exurbia trend Republican due to these beliefs in small and efficient government. Some are socially progressive, but when presented with Libertarian candidates, ex-urban residents prefer Conservative Libertarians or Constitutionalists.

Rural

Aside from exurbs, Libertarian and minor party candidates are most likely to win in rural communities. The weakness of Republican and Democratic party machines and the ability of candidates to meet each voter face-to-face are important factors. Many Independents who run in rural communities are either well-known or come from recognized families who have lived in the area for generations. In these cases, party identification is not as important as the individual candidate. In many of the local, rural communities, the office may even be non-partisan.

Please note: If you currently live in a rural community, ask yourself one question: Do I, or does my family, know almost everyone who lives here? If you have lived in the area your entire life and the answer is no, you may actually live in a newly formed exurb. If your answer is no because you are new to the area, you will be running at a disadvantage. It is doubly important that you have a very active public life and meet your constituents in person.

The success of Independents in rural communities bodes well for the future. Independent candidates in small towns have demonstrated time and again that if a voter is able to actually meet and speak with a real live Independent or minor party candidate, they can and will change their history of voting for another party. This book will benefit the residents of these rural communities the most since they are unlikely to meet a better prepared opponent.

Step 13

Advertise My Answer

Paid advertising is any piece of promotional material for your campaign including print, audio, video, and website information produced to influence public opinion. Paid advertising differs from earned media in that it is produced, distributed, and paid for directly by the campaign. You earn the earned media by doing something that is deemed newsworthy. This is also called free media.

Saturation and Cross-Confirmation

The goal of paid advertising is to attract the attention of three consumer groups: contributors, volunteers, and your voters. Keep these three groups in mind when designing your campaign material. **Contributors** want to know that their money is well-spent in a productive fashion that furthers the cause of your campaign. **Volunteers** want to join a cause greater than themselves and improve their communities. **Your voters**, those who will vote for you or could be swayed, want to know that you have their best interests at heart with the best ideas and qualifications. We will refer to these groups as consumers of your message.

There are four principal methods to deliver this message to these groups: web-based, print, audio, and video advertising. **Saturation** indicates the amount of advertising a particular consumer has received from a particular method without diminishing returns. Saturation is a subjective term that often changes from race to race and person to person.

It is subjective because it is exceedingly difficult for a low budget campaign to determine when diminishing returns begin. For example, you have probably seen a particular television commercial you thought was very amusing. You enjoyed the first few times you saw it, but didn't remember the brand being advertised. Then you noticed the brand and considered purchasing the product. You went to the store and either decided to buy it or stick with your old brand. You continue to see the commercial and now begin to find yourself irritated. It's not so funny any more. That ad not only reached saturation, but you began to feel over-saturated. At some point, you may even make a permanent decision to never buy that product because the advertising is driving you crazy. In a perfect advertising world, the commercial would have stopped when you made your decision. That would have been the moment of **perfect saturation**.

Cross-confirmation happens when you receive the same information from various sources. Your mind has a tendency to accept information that has been repeated in more than one place. For example, you watch the morning news and you hear that a particular toy is popular for Christmas and may soon sell out. Your child asks you for the toy. You are driving to work and the radio announces that Geoffrey the Giraffe will be at Toys "R" Us this weekend. You receive a flyer in the mail with a coupon. When you check your email, there is a reminder of Geoffrey's visit to Toys "R" Us. Chances are very high that you will decide to go buy a toy for your child that weekend. Every new source of information confirms itself with everything else you have seen. Cross-confirmation can be expensive and complicated to coordinate, but it is tremendously valuable. All these different materials had to come to the attention of a parent with a child of the correct age, and it was no accident they came to you.

Now obviously, you want both saturation and cross-confirmation to occur in your campaign. That is why fundraising is so essential. You will be able to get as much saturation and cross-confirmation as you can afford or the talent of your communications director can provide. Your earned media will hopefully saturate your newspaper and television news. In your paid media, your first goal is saturation in one field at a time. This book begins with the least expensive form of paid media and continues from there. You need to saturate each level of paid media before you move on to the next level.

When you determine the level of time and money to spend in each kind of advertising, you must first make your best estimate at saturation and cross-confirmation. For example, you may have ten thousand dollars to spend on paid advertising. This could be enough money to send everyone in your small district two professional mailings. You could send three mailings to every registered voter. You could send four nice mailings to every registered voter who has voted in the last four years. You could send five professional mailings to every registered voter who has voted in the last two years. You could send six mailings to every registered Democrat who voted in the last two years, or even twenty mailings to only Independents.

Given your situation, you may choose any of these options, but clearly sending one mailing to every resident is too diffuse and will reach too many non-voters. Likewise, sending twenty mailings to only Independents is over-saturation and too focused on voters who have already made their decision. You need to find the perfect of balance of reaching enough voters with sufficient repetition.

Narrowcasting

Narrowcasting refers to advertising that can be custom designed and specifically directed to a single person or family. When you send mail or make a telephone call, only that particular household will receive that particular message.

Print

The most effective and cost efficient way for local campaigns to advertise in print is through direct mail. Direct mail, like most advertising, is in a process of continual change to attract the attention of consumers bombarded by advertising. Most consultants now agree that the old-fashioned tri-fold brochure is a thing of the past. The best way for you to design your campaign materials is to start your own collection of junk mail. Every time you see a different style of junk mail, save it in a special bag or box tucked away in a closet. After you have a sizable collection, have a meeting with your family and friends. Vote on and discuss which piece has the best design and why. When designing a piece of direct mail, you have two goals. First, get the consumers' attention. Second, deliver a clear message. A good rule of thumb is to send three pieces of direct mail to your undecided voters in the last two weeks of the campaign.

There are several pieces of information your direct mail must have. There is generally a legal disclaimer requirement for all paid advertising. This disclaimer usually reads, "Paid for and Authorized by the Friends of John Smith Committee, Fred Jones, Treasurer." Do not copy this disclaimer. You must find the correct disclaimer information at your local Elections Office. You should also include all of your contact information including the name of your committee, address, phone number, fax number, email, and website.

The *I CAN* Network includes many excellent graphic designers and printers who can design and ship your pieces anywhere in the United States.

Other Printed Materials

There are other assorted printed materials necessary for your campaign: business cards, stationary, signs, bumper stickers, lapel stickers, t-shirts, and other promotional items. Once you register your name as a candidate, you will likely receive all types of brochures regarding campaign materials. It definitely pays in the long run to find low-cost suppliers. The *I CAN* network includes printers who offer low prices to liberty-minded candidates. It is also a good idea to work with local suppliers if feasible. Do not start buying just any materials without a plan. Remember there are tricks you can use to extend the life of the products you distribute. For example, refrigerator magnets with your logo name and the local football schedule are more likely to find their ways into kitchens.

Before you begin, get together your logo, campaign name, and campaign colors. Your campaign logo should be simple and easy to read. The colors are important only in that they are legible and not obnoxious or have any hidden meaning in your community. Stick to standard dark colors such as red, blue, or green. Stay away from light colors: yellow, pink and pastels. Choose carefully; once you start printing you need to stay with the same colors and logo in each promotional item you produce. Your goal is to generate name recognition, and you can't do that unless all your materials are consistently the same. It doesn't hurt to get some professional advice from the printer or an advertising friend on professional designs. Looking at other candidates' materials with a critical eye can help you design your own.

In recent years, it has become possible to produce a great deal of promotional material on your home computer and printer. On some items, this may prove cost efficient. Be sure to calculate and compare costs before you start. For example, business cards can now be made by computer quite professionally, but you will need such a large number of cards (thousands) that it is not cost efficient. Letterhead stationary is quite easily produced when you print your letter, but again, not if you are printing thousands of copies. Items such as buttons, iron-on t-shirts, labels, and stickers can all be made at home. Figure out how many you will need and get quotes from at least three vendors before making a decision. Again, all these items need to keep the same logo and color theme.

On Election Day, signs need to be posted as closely as legally possible to all polling locations. It is a good idea to do this early on Election morning just before the precincts open. This prevents signs from being stolen.

Email

Emails are the least expensive and timeliest method of consumer contact. Your campaign should make every effort to gather emails from everyone who has any contact with your campaign. Emails should be divided into mailing lists for: contributors, volunteers, staff, reporters, etc. Be sure to consult a mass email professional or an experienced volunteer for the best look, content, and method.

Use email to keep your supporters excited and informed, solicit financial contributions, and encourage and direct volunteer efforts. Feel free to email your supporters regularly, as often as once per week is not unexpected.

In some cases, your local or state Elections Office may actually provide lists of voter emails. You should send emails to all the voters in your district, but remember to use this list sparingly. Ask them for their vote and direct them towards your website. Remember that many people will consider this email as spam, and you should never ask for contributions or abuse your general voter email list. Promptly remove anyone who requests removal from your email list. Don't use it more than three times in one election cycle, and save it for the most important messages.

Audio Advertising

Your phone volunteers are your best resource for reaching every voter multiple times. There is a certain psychology to telephone volunteers. They work best in groups in phone banks. A phone bank can be as simple as several folding tables surrounded by chairs and a multitude of phone lines. There are now many kinds of cable, Internet, and virtual phone companies, so check around. Another option is inviting volunteers with free weekend and night minutes on their cell phones to come in. Be sure to give the volunteers scripts and talking points. Phone volunteers can be used to target different types of voters with your different messages, fundraise, organize rides for GOTV, and remind your favorables to vote on Election Day.

Another inexpensive way to reach your voters is with taped phone messages, also known as "robo-calls." As of this writing, prices as low as five cents per call are not uncommon. There are different options available for phone messages. It is recommended that you use a service that detects the beep of an answering machine and only leaves messages on machines. Don't abuse this method, as most people have a low tolerance for such advertising. Calling voters more than twice in four months is not recommended. Remember that politicians excluded themselves from the telemarketing do not call list. Your campaign can call anyone. But if you get a complaint, mark that person as "do not call" on your voter database.

Broadcasting

Broadcasting refers to advertising that will be seen or heard by everyone in your community such as newspaper, radio, and television.

Most local campaigns will not be managing budgets large enough to justify newspaper advertising. In the case of small town, locally owned non-dailies, it may be a good idea to buy a couple reasonably priced ads. It may provide some cross-confirmation, but more importantly, you'll improve your relations with the editor.

Local AM radio stations are often an effective low cost method of advertising. Radios and television stations must offer politicians their lowest unit rate and cannot deny you advertising time as long as spots are available. The lowest unit rate is the cheapest possible ad price usually reserved for large advertisers who buy in bulk, but are made available to political campaigns by law. AM radio stations are usually very helpful and will often produce your ad for free or at very little cost.

You or your communications director need to write your copy before you go to the station. Feel free to ask the station personnel for help.

In whatever audio advertising you choose, you need to saturate your medium. However many ads you can afford to purchase, keep them close together and on the same days. Talk to your station personnel about saturation levels and ad rotation schedules.

Choose which stations you advertise with based on their audience demographics. Remember what we said in Step 9: older, wealthier home and business owners are the most likely to vote. People who attend church are also more likely to vote. Christian radio stations are a good buy for most candidates. It all depends on the specifics of your race.

Most local campaigns will not have a budget for broadcast television advertising. Remember that you need to saturate every level of advertising you purchase. Television saturation is measured in a point system and varies according to market. You do not want to project an unprofessional image by creating a low-budget TV ad. If you only air it a few times, it will have no measurable impact on your campaign, but will cost thousands of dollars.

Cable television is much more affordable and is much more targeted. Like radio, cable TV has a multitude of specific channels that offer you many opportunities to target specific demographic groups. Decide what your target is and ask the cable folks to help you target them. FYI: Independent voters watch a lot of Science Fiction, so the SciFi channel is an excellent buy.

Roadside signs are a large project that should be managed by a particularly handy and reliable volunteer. All sign locations need to be recorded for future pick-up. Many municipalities have deadlines and fines for sign take-downs or lack thereof. **Beware the sign wars**. In recent years, the number of citizens and campaigns stealing each other's signs has reached a fever pitch. Do not retaliate in kind. The very best way to deal with this problem is to video tape the perpetrator and give the tape to your local news stations and papers. This will devastate your opponent. As a general rule, signs need to be posted on private property with the owner's permission and should not be staked in public right of way alongside roads.

Website

Every candidate must have a website. It has become expected and unavoidable. Since it is considered so easy and cheap, not having a website raises serious concerns about whether a campaign is "for real." The first thing nearly every consumer tells a candidate is, "Everything you say sounds great. Is there a website where I can get more information?" Most consumers now prefer to get at least some of their information from the web.

There are several functions a good website can perform for your campaign. First, it can be an electronic brochure and newsletter (but this should not be its only purpose). Portions of your website should include a candidate bio and resume, your campaign message, and your three most important issues. Web space is cheap, but avoid including too much information. You can't be all things to all people. Remember, the first two people who will read your website are your opponent and his manager. Don't give them ammunition.

Create a page specifically for the media and clearly label it as such on your homepage. The media need high resolution photos that can be downloaded. Be sure to include your headshot, action shots with you meeting voters, and family pictures. You can also post all your press releases on this page and examples of media stories already written about your campaign.

Make your website interesting, but don't get so flashy it dazes or confuses voters. Some websites look like a herd of zebras running in different directions. Don't do that. The website's home page should include content that changes on a regular basis. The easiest way to do this is to have a section for press releases, campaign progress reports, and any media stories written about you. Have downloadable audio and video clips from recent campaign events.

Make sure that you have a method for accepting financial contributions online. There are many websites to securely collect contributions. I still recommend PayPal, even though their customer service can be exasperating. Whatever service you choose, pick a site that quickly makes your money available at your request. In a local campaign, you can't wait a month for a check to come in from a website. This method of contributing money is now very popular. It is the most cost effective method of collecting money for your campaign. More and more people every day are becoming comfortable with sending money online. The best thing about online fundraising is the immediate gratification. The second a person feels excited about your message, they are able to contribute. It can be spontaneous, instantly completed, and credited to your account. When you appear on television, make sure your web address is visible on your podium or in the background.

Gathering volunteer contact information is another important goal of your website. Your webmaster should know how to set up fields for volunteers to type their information. Ask them what type of activity they want to perform, just as you would on a traditional volunteer form. Whenever you meet a new contact during your campaign, be sure to get their email, and type it into your database. You should send all your contacts regular campaign updates with a financial contribution button. Regarding spam complaints, it is much easier to beg forgiveness than ask for permission. If someone doesn't want your updates, politely respond and remove them from your email list. Asking if someone wants to be on your update list is like asking for your first kiss. It spoils the spontaneity.

There is a list of website design tips in the *18 Steps to Win a Local Election Workbook*.

Social Networking on the Web

Social networking has recently become the number one activity on the Internet. As of this printing, websites such as **Facebook**, **Meetup**, **LinkedIn**, **Twitter**, **YouTube**, and **Flickr** have become new ways for people to meet and organize their social and professional lives. New social networks are popping up everyday and are becoming more specialized. These websites have combined in unexpected ways and will continue to transform the way people organize themselves.

Twitter is essentially a miniature blog. You (or your social networking volunteer) can continuously update your **Twitter** "followers" on your campaign and the candidate's daily schedule. Make sure that you can update your **Twitter** status from your cell phone. You can send "tweets" in your down time about where you are going or what you are doing at that moment. **Twitter** is an important "top of the mind" form of advertising. This means that your followers are thinking about you every time you tweet (multiple times per day). This helps your volunteers and contributors feel like they are more involved in the campaign. It also demonstrates how busy you are and how much you are doing to advance the cause. You can send **Twitter** updates automatically to change your Facebook status; that's a great two for one combination.

Facebook can transform your personal and professional life. It helps you maintain and grow your network of friends by making it very easy to share your ideas, plans, and interesting news articles. **Facebook** makes it fun and easy to organize political groups, events, and causes. By using the advertising feature, you can focus your paid advertising on people who live in a specific area and have profiles containing keywords like "Ron Paul," "Libertarian," "Ayn Rand," or "Constitution." **Facebook** can accept automatic feeds from **Twitter**, **Meetup**, and other sites. Be sure to take advantage of this feature. Take your time to explore the **Facebook** website and its options. They are constantly adding new free and paid features.

Meetup is very useful for planning events and organizing like-minded people. When you set up your **Meetup** group, be sure to select a wide range of keywords so that you can be found by like-minded people. You don't have to agree 100% with everyone who may be interested in your campaign, so include keywords like "Libertarian," "U.S. Constitution," "Ron Paul," "Glen Beck," and "Tea Parties." After you setup your group, **Meetup** will notify everyone in your community who has expressed an interest in your keywords, so you want to be as broad as possible. You can schedule events, collect pre-paid RSVP's, share pictures, and many other things on **Meetup**. You can also send automatic **Meetup** updates to your **Facebook** profile, and even your online campaign calendar. It is well worth the current monthly fee.

LinkedIn is geared more towards finding a new job, posting your resume, and getting recommendations from former colleagues and supervisors. You can use this site to maintain your professional contacts. Don't be afraid to ask for recommendations. You can always delete those comments you dislike.

Youtube is an essential website for sharing your campaign videos. You can set up your own **Youtube** campaign channel, and your friends can subscribe for updates. **Youtube** makes it very easy to post videos to your own website and to share videos on **Facebook** and **Twitter**. They are constantly updating this site, so be sure to look at all the features.

Flickr is a great way for your friends, campaign staff, volunteers, and even the general public to share high resolution photos. You can set up a group just for your campaign pictures.

Remember, the best way to take full advantage of social networking websites is to combine all of them with your campaign website. Some people will prefer one over others, but you need to be ready and flexible to use them all to reach your audience. If you are not adept at social networking, find a good volunteer who is.

❦ Step 14 ❧

Become the News

To become the news, you must do, say, or expose newsworthy stories. This may sound obvious, but most candidates who fail to get good headlines are often not doing anything interesting enough to merit headlines.

If you are running a micro-campaign for the township water board or planning commission, you may only get two mentions in the paper: once when you declare, and once when you win. But you can turn this around by doing your own research and writing news releases that tell interesting stories.

It is possible that your local news may have some interest in suppressing your candidacy. You can, however, overcome this tendency by creating such interesting news events and stories that the media can no longer afford to ignore you. Always remember that the news media is in the sales business. Are you the proverbial Eskimo selling ice or Evel Knievel jumping over a hundred buses?

Public Announcement

After carefully crafting a campaign message, you are now ready to make your first public announcement. Set a time and place for your announcement. Look for a slow news day such as Wednesday or Thursday and check to make sure there are no important publicly scheduled events that conflict. This will help you get maximum coverage in the news. You should also check with your closest supporters to be sure they are available to attend your announcement.

Draft a statement and share it with your campaign manager and close confidantes. Have your campaign manager or media consultant issue a press release. Notify your local and state party. They can serve as volunteers during your announcement and help you explain the philosophy of your party.

Your public announcement is the first major milestone in your campaign. As such, make it a special event for your friends and family. Your announcement should happen in a very public or professional place. It may be outside in the center of your local downtown, inside a private room rented in a restaurant or hotel, or at your campaign headquarters, if suitable. Invite all your contacts by telephone and your VIP's by written invitation. It's a great idea to schedule a party for your guests immediately following the announcement. Nothing attracts people like the prospect of free food, but don't get too fancy. Your printed fundraising materials should be ready and distributed. Remind your guests that in order to be successful, you will need both money and volunteers. Your finance director should remind them of the costs of putting this event together.

Public Relations Disaster

This is a cautionary tale that highlights the importance of professional public relations.

Sammith Thammasaroj was head of Thailand's meteorological agency in the 1990's. He warned the public about the danger of tsunamis and lobbied the government for the creation of a tsunami early warning system. Thailand had never been affected by a tsunami in modern times, and his system was rejected. One day, he received unconfirmed data suggesting an imminent tsunami was about reach Thailand. He alerted the public. When the giant wave failed to arrive, he was fired from his position and humiliated.

In 2004, Suparek Thantiratanawong, the new head of meteorology in Thailand received confirmed data from reputable sources that his country was about to be swamped in a massive tidal wave. Remembering the fate of his former boss, he did not publicize the information. Over a hundred thousand people died due to poor public relations.

Three mistakes were made: 1) Sammith was unable to convince his government to install an early warning system. 2) Sammith used unreliable data to issue a press release that proved false, utterly destroying his credibility. 3) Following his predecessor, Suparek did not have the confidence to issue a press release based on proven facts.

This is an old story known as crying wolf. As a responsible and professional candidate, you hold your own credibility and that of your party or fellow Independents in your hands. Hopefully, no mistake on your part will ever cause such a horrible disaster, but you could easily set back the cause of liberty in your community.

Major Daily Newspapers and News Services

In every major city, there is usually one major daily newspaper that dominates the media market and sets the tone for news in your region. Unfortunately, most Americans no longer get their news from physical newspapers, but your relations with the newspaper are very important in shaping the coverage you receive from other news organizations.

Television news and the news wire services such as Reuters and the Associated Press will immediately pick up any story published in your major daily newspaper. Your local broadcast television may decide to pass on the story, but they will be aware of it. Thus, it is essential to have good relations with any major daily paper if you live within its market.

Most newspapers are now owned by large media conglomerates such as Gannett and have been substantially downsized and streamlined. Other newspapers have been able to stay independent, but also downsized in order to compete. This means that reporters work on very strict schedules and deadlines. Your job as a candidate or campaign manager is to make a reporter's job to cover you as easy as possible. This means writing and distributing press releases which can be used nearly word for word. If you write the article in the same style as the newspaper and include some contrary viewpoints, you may find your entire release cut and pasted into tomorrow's paper.

Typically, your paper will assign one or possibly two political reporters to cover your race. It is important for you to meet these reporters early and establish trust. You can normally predict who these reporters will be by reading similar political stories from your neighborhood and checking the bylines. Find out how the reporter prefers to receive your press releases. Most prefer faxes or emails. Always call your reporter to be sure a news release has been received, especially faxes. You may also ask if he is able to come to your scheduled press conference. Offer to change your schedule if there is a conflict, as it is likely you will also lose your television stations if another event is trumping your own. There are suggestions on how to develop good relations with the media at the end of this section.

Television News

The key to television news is usually the assignment desk. The assignment desk is responsible for sending reporters and cameras into the field. Your challenge is to convince the assignment editor that your news is among the most important of the day and deserves coverage. Keep in mind that your event will require the television station to send a camera crew. This is expensive, and stations typically have only one to three crews available on any given day. If you waste their time, you may never get a second opportunity. The farther your scheduled event is from the station, the less likely a crew will come to your event. Most crews will travel a half hour with no problem.

Your best chance to get television time is to schedule your event for a slow news day. Wednesdays and Thursdays are typically the slowest, but check around with other reporters and call the assignment desk to see if another time may be better. More information on holding a press conference appears later in this chapter.

Non-Daily Newspapers

Most small towns and suburbs have weekly, bi-weekly, and monthly publications. These newspapers can be associated with a major daily, part of a conglomerate, or independent operations. There are a few subtle differences to keep in mind during your campaign.

If the paper is associated with a major daily, the political reporter may be the same person. If the paper is part of a conglomerate, there may be only one very busy reporter who covers politics in several towns and counties. If the paper is locally owned and operated, the editor and political reporter may be the same person. Always visit locally operated non-dailies in person to introduce yourself. You may also wish to indicate your interest in buying advertising and how much you're planning to spend. This will do wonders for your local coverage.

Radio Stations

Most radio stations do not have stand-alone news operations. If a radio station is part of a larger broadcast company, the television news people may broadcast on their channel. Otherwise, most radio stations simply read the news from the AP wire service or even from the newspaper.

The exception is the public radio station. If you live near a large city, you will probably have a few reporters at a local public radio station. There may also be talk radio broadcast in your area. It is usually a great idea to appear on your local talk radio station, but be sure the host is at least somewhat favorable to your cause. Otherwise, you can find yourself insulted and interrupted with no way to defend yourself. Most talk radio thrives on controversy, so be careful.

Alternative Media Outlets

Independent and minor party candidates generally do very well with alternative media outlets.

Alternative Newspapers

There are two types of alternative newspapers. These are often called major and minor alternative papers. The first type is usually a large tabloid newspaper distributed for free in large urban markets. These newspapers focus on alternative lifestyle issues, sexual and gay rights, civil liberties, rock music, movies, extreme sports, and city politics. These newspapers often understand Independents and are willing to spare more ink and space for their issues. In some cases, Independents have been given the opportunity to publish regular columns and headlines on the front page. Unfortunately, the readership is less likely to vote than that of more mainstream newspapers. It is still important to make an effort with these newspapers because coverage in one paper makes you newsworthy for other publications.

Another type of alternative newspaper is printed in the garages and apartments of students and other activists across America. These are essentially amateur writers who publish for a particular cause or group as a hobby. They have very small circulations but their readers are very loyal fans. These papers can give you some practice answering interviews and are often surprisingly objective. Getting a story in this kind of newspaper can give you some "street cred" and may lead to publication in your area's major alternative paper.

Webzines

Many alternative newspapers have stopped publishing on paper altogether and now exist completely online. Other news groups and magazines are recent upstarts and were never printed on paper. Many of your local webzines will publish your press releases with minimal or no editing. The readerships are small, but very dedicated. Some webzines are called blogs.

Weblogs or Blogs and Discussion Boards

Political weblogs became very popular at the beginning of this century. Blogs are essentially public diaries wherein a candidate or campaign staffer can write about what happened on the campaign trail each day. Some activists, supporters, and volunteers get very excited and motivated by blogs. The typical voter will spend little time if any on a local candidate's blog.

Another new phenomenon is the local political discussion board. Generally speaking, it is not a good idea for a candidate to respond to political discussions on boards. It is easy to spend a lot of time responding to these boards, and their readers are generally already decided voters. Blogs and discussion boards have a tendency to attract people who think alike and are very difficult to influence. Monitoring or maintaining weblogs and discussion boards is a good job for a volunteer who works from home. Do not let the opinions of a few local bloggers interfere with your overall campaign strategy unless they point out a true weakness or oversight in the campaign.

Bloggers and discussion board members who agree with your campaign should be invited to your events. Many of them enjoy the opportunity to meet in person and may decide to become active in your campaign. Some bloggers are also amateur journalists and enjoy interviewing candidates. Humor their interests as long as it does not interfere with your campaign schedule. They are a small but potentially influential group. Publication in a blog or discussion board can occasionally lead to newsworthiness and more coverage in major periodicals.

Developing Contacts

Cultivating media contacts is simpler than it may appear. There are many methods, but here are some suggestions.

Before you ever decide to run for office, volunteer to be your organization's media contact. This works especially well if you are involved in a charitable service organization like the Lion's Club or Kiwanis. Even if you are only representing your local Independent group or minor party, this is appropriate.

Make an appointment to visit your local small town editor or political reporter. Be punctual for your meeting. Media people work on deadlines. Introduce yourself and the organization you represent. Explain what activities and events your group is currently sponsoring. Bring some information, either a brochure or some other type of handout for the reporter to keep. It is even better if you assemble a complete media kit.

Inform the contact about your commitment to the community and your desire to develop better relations between your organization and his newspaper. Ask the editor or reporter if there is anything you can do to help improve your organization's contact with the paper. Be sure to exchange business cards and ask the reporter or editor the best method for submitting press releases and meeting times from your organization. Take written notes of your conversation, and thank everyone for their time.

Assemble a professional media kit. Media kits are usually made with paper folders with pockets. You must also make your media kit available for download on your website. You should create one for both your organization and your campaign. Your campaign media kit should include: a candidate bio, a statement of your campaign theme and three most important issues, a physical and electronic copy of your professional headshot, a physical and electronic copy of several good action shots, your campaign promotional materials, and contact information for the candidate and your communication's director. Definitely include your cell phone number. Media calls can come at any time and must be answered immediately. For safety reasons, do not publish your home address. This is one reason why you need a campaign office or at least a P.O. box.

News releases should be direct, written in the same style as a newspaper article, and tell a story of conflict interesting to the reader. Include several quotes for and against your main story.

Campaign Logo Goes Here
Campaign Address, Website
Date

FOR IMMEDIATE RELEASE

NEWS RELEASE (or NEWS CONFERENCE)

Contact: Communication Director's Name
(Office) (123) 456-7890
(Cell) (123) 456-7890
Email: communications@campaign.org

TIME: (Date and Time of New Conference)
LOCATION: (Location of News Conference)

MAIN TITLE OF NEWS RELEASE IN CAPS
Subheading in Upper and Lower Case

This sentence grabs attention with a clear statement of bold action from candidate. This sentence adds some details. Adds some details.

"A visionary candidate quote," said the candidate.

More details about the story. More details about the story. More details about the story. More details about the story.

"Someone with a weak contrary view is quoted here."

More details about the story. More details about the story.

"Candidate slams the door on the weak argument. Candidate does not personally attack speaker of argument."

"Campaign Manager says campaign is the best thing since sliced bread."

# # #

Organizing a News Conference

The type of race you are running will determine the number and frequency of your news conferences. Micro-campaigns for a water or land use planning board may attract very little attention, and races for city council or mayor may attract a great deal of media scrutiny. Whether your race is large or small, you definitely want to organize a news conference for your announcement. This may be your only news conference in a micro-campaign. Unless you discover real evidence of a major scandal, micro-campaigns attract mostly print news. Due to the rise of electronic and television news, press releases and press conferences are often called news releases and news conferences. They are the same thing. Professionalism with the news media is vital. Every contact you have, and especially news conferences, should be professionally and carefully managed.

Candidates for mayor or city council typically generate much more publicity even in small towns. One press release per week and one conference per month are not unusual. When you or your manager have multiple story ideas, be sure to pace your media stories to keep up a steady rhythm of news from your campaign. Avoid the temptation to write or say too many ideas in one release. Keep the focus on one news item at a time. Too much information will sound jumbled and confusing for your readers, and the intent of your message will be lost.

A news conference is called when a story is so big that a simple release is not enough. As the candidate or manager, it is your responsibility to generate big stories and keep your campaign interesting for both the media and your voters. You or your manager should already have a list of phone numbers, fax number, and emails for each reporter or news organizations in your area. Be sure to send faxes and call the principals to make sure they received the fax. Failure to call will result in no-shows and low attendance.

Your press conference notice looks like a normal press release and outlines the story for the conference. The only difference is in your subject line and headline. For example: type "News Conference" across the top instead of "News Release," and change your headline to: "Branson Calls News Conference, Accuses Mayor of Running Up City Debt." Remember that your press conferences should be fun and exciting. Invite and encourage all of your volunteers to be present and act as your cheerleaders. Volunteers should wear their campaign t-shirts, if possible.

Tell a Visual Story

Remember that pictures speak louder than words on television. First, be sure you choose a location easily accessible to the media and that helps in telling your story. For example, if your conference concerns eminent domain, have the press conference in front of the homes to be torn down. Speak from behind a handsome wooden podium. Have a flag or city emblem visible. Scout your location in advance. Pay very close attention to what appears behind you in the camera shot; is it the image you want for yourself and this story? When learning about visual imagery on television, watch your local news with the sound muted. What are the pictures you see? What does the background convey? Is it quiet enough for television and radio audio? Attention to visual detail is what separates the great orators from the average politicians, and your television media will love you for it.

Tell a Spoken Story

Write down what you have to say in advance, and memorize it until you're comfortable to speak without notes. Have an outline of your main points in an oversized font at your podium. Be sure to start with a few short punchy sentences that encapsulate everything you want your audience to understand. Develop a sentence rhythm: short, short, long, short, short, long. This kind of sentence pattern is pleasing to the ear. Have residents ready to give their stories. Be sure to have any speeches or testimony written and give copies to all the media present. Be sure to list the names of everyone who will be speaking and their titles or relevance to the story.

Your campaign manager or communications director should stand behind the cameras and reporters to offer direction to the candidate if needed. For example, a manager may hastily scribble SPEAK INTO THE MIC in large block letters on a sheet of paper or MENTION THE HOSPITAL. The manager or director should hold this note in the air behind the cameras and reporters. Do not pass notes to the front, this is distracting for the audience and the candidate. Work out hand signals in advance so that your manager can give immediate feedback while you're speaking.

If you are accusing a public official or board of misconduct, financial trouble, or any kind of scandal, be ready to provide copies of your evidence at your conference. Fully explain the accusation and demonstrate your evidence. Anticipate any excuse your opponent may use and discredit this excuse in advance. As an Independent, you must be prepared to be charged as a "conspiracy theorist" or simply "a nut." Unfortunately, Independents and minor party candidates have a history of making accusations without proof. If you do this, you will lose your credibility, and no one will ever come to another news conference or print your releases. As my mother used to say, "When you point your finger, three of your own fingers are pointing back." Be careful with accusations and never make them personal. Never insult your opponent or make disparaging comments; they will reflect poorly on your professionalism and your ability to effectively solve public problems.

News Release vs. Letter to the Editor

It is very common for new or amateur campaign managers or communications directors to confuse a news release with an opinion piece. You can send your opinions to the editors of newspapers in your area. Just be sure to clearly label them as "Letters to the Editor," not "News Release."

News releases contain a new story about some new action the candidate is taking. For example: "Candidate Bob Smith Proposes New Budget Plan to Cut Taxes." This is an action taken by the candidate to solve a problem. **Letters to the Editor, Blogs, or Op-Ed columns** are written to express opinions: "Candidate Bob Smith Doesn't Like Taxes." This is an opinion, not an action. And it is not "news" that a politician says he doesn't like taxes. A winning campaign *does* *something* to solve community issues, it doesn't just complain. If you want to become the news, you must act on the local stage, not opine.

Follow-up

After your speech or announcement, the reporters will generally ask follow-up questions. Try to anticipate these questions and practice answering them with your manager. Remember that television reporters are looking for sound bites and print reporters are looking for good turns of phrase. Both require simple answers to complicated questions. After the conference, reporters may want to speak with your manager or volunteers for different points of view. Prepare your volunteers, but not too much. Reporters may decide not to use any comments that sound rehearsed. An hour after everyone has left, your manager or director should call the reporters and ask them if they have all the quotes and information they need. You may also ask when they anticipate the story to be released on the air or in the paper.

"Off the Record"

If you're doing a good job with the media, you will soon develop special relationships. Reporters commonly want to know the "whole story" about what's going on behind the scenes of your campaign or the interactions you have with your supporters or your opponent. Sometimes reporters will privately ask you questions you may not want to answer publicly. You have to balance your campaign's need for privacy and your relationship with your reporters. This is when you may decide to answer questions "off the record."

You must clearly state that your answer is "off the record" and hear your reporter's consent. Your reporter will put his hands down and stop taking notes or recording. Remember that you are taking a calculated risk. Reporters have been known to gossip and even publicly report items said in confidence. If a reporter publicly reports an "off the record" answer, he knows he may forever lose your trust and possibly the trust of others. Remember that some reporters have gone to jail to protect the confidence of their informants. Don't abuse this trust.

Unfair Negativity and Errors

If a reporter abuses your trust or continually publishes unfairly negative stories about your campaign or your party, it is a good idea to speak with them about it. Be sincere and professional, never angry or emotional. You may decide to speak with the editor of the publication and/or have your supporters write letters to the editor. Remember that the media are people too. They have emotions, strict deadlines, and crazy schedules. They make mistakes sometimes. That is why you should always provide them with written material and press releases. This will hopefully avoid the most common mistakes. Try to be understanding and patient.

Publicity Events

In addition to press releases and conferences, you can generate positive publicity by attending public events. There are many types of events you can attend: local Rotary, Lions, and Kiwanis club meetings; high school and professional sporting events; professional association and union meetings; Chamber of Commerce meetings, League of Women Voters; etc.

Be sure to issue press releases and send pictures of your events to the print media and publish them on your website or blog. Some of these events will allow you to speak, and others will not. It is important for your scheduler to clarify and distinguish speaking events. Some organizations have rules against political speakers, but you can still attend as an audience member and speak with members privately. Your attention will be noted and appreciated.

High school and college social studies instructors often offer opportunities for local candidates to speak to their classes. This is a good opportunity for community outreach and to show your concern for local students. Remember that these children have parents who vote, and the students are often voting for the first time.

As an Independent or minor party candidate, you and your staff need to be extra sharp on the lookout for political debates and "meet the candidate" nights. You may not get automatically invited, so your scheduler and campaign manager need to seek this information and do their research.

Step 15

Attend Public Events

Every candidate must make every effort to appear at local forums and debates. These candidates' nights are your opportunity to reach interested voters and allow the voters to see you and your opponent together in the same room.

Before you attend any forum or debate, practice answering questions with your staff. Together, you should be able to anticipate most of the questions you will be asked. Craft the best possible answers, and practice those answers until they become second nature. Memorize specific facts and figures to back up your opinions.

Remember that you are attending this event to convey your message to the voters. We said before that the winner is the person who tells the best story to the most voters. You are here to tell your story. Make sure that is your priority. When you make your opening statements, and whenever you answer a question, be sure to tie in your unique story and background.

These events typically take place on a September or October evening at the local community center, VFW hall, or public library. It is essentially a job interview in which you and your opponent will stand side by side to appeal for votes, present your strengths, and explain your answers to local issues.

Look your best. Wear your best suit. Bring someone with you to help you carry and hand out materials. Be gracious and magnanimous to your hosts and to your opponent. Nasty or rude comments will not win votes, even if your opponent deserves them.

Bring a volunteer sign-up sheet, pledge cards, business cards, and your printed material (fliers, post cards, slim jim, etc.)

After the event is over, analyze your performance with your staff who attended the event. Did you stay on message? Did you answer the questions? Did your message resonate with the audience? Was your delivery on target? A good candidate will improve and learn from each event.

If you are an Independent or minor party candidate, make sure that these forums are aware of your campaign. If you are blocked from participating, work together with your staff and volunteers to come up with productive solutions. If a hundred people call the organization or email them to complain, they might change their minds. If you are still unable to secure an invitation, your campaign should weigh the pros and cons of staging a demonstration outside the event. Hand out specially made fliers explaining what happened and ask why you aren't being included. Hand these out in addition to your usual fliers or cards.

Step 16

Go Door-to-Door

As a local candidate, you should plan on campaigning door-to-door at least three days per week. Your scheduler should set aside time for this purpose, but stay flexible. Volunteers should accompany the candidate as much as possible. Pair volunteers of the opposite sex to walk together. Women will be hesitant to open their doors to solitary men. The first step in any door-to-door campaign is identifying and sorting communities in three sections: your favorable precincts, swing precincts, and your unfavorable precincts. The targeting section of this book describes how to identify each precinct.

Where you go depends on your campaign strategy. If you are a new, relatively unknown candidate, you will need to visit precincts you predict to be favorable to introduce yourself. This will strengthen your base and give you an idea of how favorable the precinct really is. You will also need to visit the swing precincts. This is your opportunity to convince undecided or otherwise persuadable voters. Swing voters and Independents vote for candidates, not parties, so you have an excellent chance to win their votes.

You should only visit unfavorable neighborhoods if you have time and only after visiting the favorable and swing precincts. If you are running in a two-way campaign, consider that most voters of the other party will break your way if you can get them to the polling place. For example, when running against a Republican, approach Democrats in your door-to-door campaign sympathetically. Be sure they know you are the only non-Republican choice and convince them of your value as a candidate.

After you have decided which neighborhoods to walk, assemble your walking list before you go out. The walking list should have been printed on labels and stuck to index cards or sheets of paper. These index cards will have some questions you would like to ask each voter. An easy way to make your own question cards is with a photocopier and cardstock. Your questions should have something to do with your message and help you identify issues important to your community. Feedback received from your door-to-door campaign should be used to refine your message. In some cases, you and your manager may decide to change your message completely. This should be done if it has no traction with your voters.

Questions should be yes or no, or positive or negative. For example: How do you feel about our mayor? Do you think it was a good idea for the mayor to borrow a hundred million dollars for the new city hall? You definitely want to ask how people feel about your opponent and why. The answers on your card will be a scale from one to five. A one indicates highly negative, a two: somewhat negative, a three: neutral or doesn't know, a four: somewhat positive, and a five: highly positive. Circle the name of the voter you spoke to, or write his or her name if not listed. Correct your cards if the voter listed has died or moved. Be sure to get the new names. This data is extremely important and valuable to your campaign as well as to your local and state parties. Take the time to get it right.

When you are finished walking for the day, gather your data and that of your volunteers. Give your cards to your database person or the designated organizer right away. These cards have a tendency to get lost or out of order if not taken care of immediately. This information can be used in many ways. First, you now have data which enables you to target voters at the individual level. You can customize your mailings. It is especially important to stop wasting time and money on decided voters. People who love and like you need to be saved for get out the vote. Continue mailing and phoning your positives; you don't want them to forget you. People who hate and dislike you should be removed from future mailings and phone calls. In aggregate, these numbers can give you the pulse of the community. It is important that you check voters' responses to your message. If they seem apathetic or hostile to your message, then you need to find out why and fix it.

~ Step 17 ~

Get Out the Vote

Getting out the vote, or GOTV, refers to all the activity conducted by your campaign to ensure that your supporters get to the polling places on Election Day to vote for you. If your campaign has followed the previous 16 Steps, you should have a valuable database of all the voters in your precincts, and you have some idea of who is voting for you. There is documented evidence that well-conducted GOTV operations will boost your vote totals. Tremendously well-orchestrated GOTV efforts were credited with saving George Bush's narrow victories in 2000 and 2004. But for the local candidate, they are especially effective in small, off-year elections and during bad weather when many people put off voting.

Phone Operation

Over the course of your campaign, you have identified who will vote for you on a scale of one to five. You have also identified supporters who need a ride to the polls on Election Day. Four days before Election Day, your volunteers need to begin calling those who need a ride to confirm a time and place for pick-up. Here is a sample script. Feel free to alter the script to meet the circumstances of your campaign.

> **Volunteer:** *Hello. This is _____ calling on behalf of Fred Jones for Mayor. According to our records, you indicated you may need a ride on Election Day. Your vote is important. Do you need any assistance getting to the polls on this Tuesday?*

(If yes): *We have volunteers who have offered to drive people to the polls on Election Day. I would be happy to schedule a driver to pick you up. Can you please tell me when would be a good time? And where should our driver meet you? OK. We will be sending a driver at (time)_____ on Election Day to meet you at (address)_____.*

Do you have a pen handy? Please call _____ if you have any questions or need to cancel or change your pick-up. Thank you for your time. Have a good day.

(If no): *We have plenty of volunteers who would be happy to help you. Are you sure you can get to the polls OK? Alright, can I give you our phone number in case you change your mind? It's _____. Have a nice day.*

On the day before the election, your volunteers should begin calling all likely voters who scored favorable to your campaign. Remind them to vote on Election Day. If your phone volunteers run through their list, they can call a second time.

Volunteer: *Hello. This is _____ calling on behalf of Fred Jones for Mayor. Your vote is very important to our campaign. We feel we have a good chance to make a strong showing in this election, but we really need you to go vote this Tuesday for Fred Jones. Can we count on your vote?*

(If yes): *Do you need a ride to your polling place?* **(If yes see above).** *Thank you for your support. Have a great day.*

On Election Day

On Election Day, you've finally reached the last inning, but don't take your eye off the ball. There are several simple, but complicated operations that need to go smoothly. Be sure your volunteer coordinator has everything in hand or receives proper help. Every person in the campaign should plan to spend most, if not all, of their day at a precinct polling place handing out palm cards or driving people to the polls. The Election Night party is the best time to thank everyone and have a good time.

The Candidate

The candidate needs to remain calm and cool during this potentially stressful day. The campaign staff should help put the candidate at ease. The candidate should vote at the opening time in his or her polling location. Send press releases the night before to all of your media contacts with a complete schedule indicating where and when the candidate will be voting, where the candidate will be during the day, and the location of your Election Night party. The candidate should plan to be at the highest priority polling location all day shaking hands and passing out palm cards.

If the weather is hot, the candidate should go home for a very quick shower at 1PM. The candidate needs to have a volunteer to assist them throughout the day and carry a cellular phone. Under no circumstances should the candidate attempt to shake hands while speaking on the phone. The candidate should be prepared to leave the polling place to do television interviews if necessary. All other interviews should be conducted by phone. After the polls close, the candidate should take a quick shower before the Election Night party. At the election party, thank all your family, friends, and supporters who have believed in you.

The Campaign Manager

The campaign manager should plan to work at the second highest priority polling location or assist in GOTV as much as possible. The manager should be sure that the Election Day operation is running smoothly and be in regular contact with the staff. This is the day for maximum delegation of authority and volunteer effort. Hold a meeting the night before the election and make sure everyone knows their designated task. The manager can't possibly do everything or be everywhere on Election Day.

The Volunteer Coordinator

This is the busiest driving day for the volunteer coordinator. They need to be sure that the phone volunteers have all the correct phone numbers they need. They need to check volunteer attendance at the precincts in person. They should also be sure the precinct volunteers have adequate signs, materials, water, and snacks. At lunch time, the coordinator should deliver lunch so that the volunteers can stay on location all day. Sometimes, campaigns use high school or college students to volunteer at polling locations. Offer these students food if you see them without it. They may switch to supporting your campaign. Many times, a business owner friendly to the campaign will provide box lunches for free or at a reduced rate for volunteers on Election Day.

Make sure the volunteer coordinator's cell phone is powered up today. Everyone should be calling in if they have any difficulty. If your volunteers have a problem with poll workers, the volunteer coordinator should check out the problem for themselves. They should see if a serious law is being broken, or if there is just a simple difference of opinion. If the problem seriously interferes with the election, and the volunteer coordinator cannot resolve the issue with the on-site leader of the poll workers, it is time to phone the elections office to notify them directly. In many cases, the poll workers are volunteers and may misunderstand the law.

The volunteer coordinator should not waste time arguing over how far volunteers are standing from the polling place. Every precinct leader seems to have a different concept of distance. As long as all the campaigns are treated equally, there isn't much you can do. Document any election irregularity. Take photos and get names.

As night approaches, the volunteer coordinator needs to prepare for the election night party. They should take a quick shower if they need it and prepare the party location. Get some volunteers to help out.

Phone Volunteers

Phone volunteers should spend the day calling registered voters who have previously indicated at least some support for your campaign. They need to remind people that today is Election Day and where they should go to vote. They should also ask if the voter needs assistance in getting to the polls.

Volunteer Drivers

Volunteer drivers are going to be the campaign's taxi/shuttle bus service. These volunteers need to be given specific instructions on when and where to pick up voters and have maps of all the polling locations. These drivers need to have radios or cell phones so they can report back to their coordinator and receive last minute information. Try to keep the drivers in the same neighboring precincts if possible. Drivers should have magnets, or some other type of identification on their cars and on their person (t-shirt or name tag). It is best to use cars or vans that are easy to enter and exit. They should be clean and professional. Keep adequate supplies of campaign materials in the vehicle for people to read and allow them to show their support with stickers.

Precinct Volunteers

Your campaign manager needs to determine which precincts have the highest priority. Working together with your volunteer coordinator, your manager should plan to have at least two volunteers at each polling place beginning with the highest priority locations. High priority precincts are determined by the number of expected voters and the expected level of support. Mixed and undecided precincts with large numbers of voters are the highest priority. Your precincts are the next highest, and your opponent's or small precincts are the lowest priority. Your volunteers will stand near the polling place, distribute literature, shake hands, and encourage people to vote for you. They should all wear a campaign t-shirt. Make sure that every volunteer knows the law concerning where to stand and what can be done on Election Day at the polling places. They should make sure that every polling place has campaign signs posted at the lawful distance. Volunteers need to remember that the official poll workers determine how the rules will be enforced.

Volunteers should never argue with a poll worker or election official. If a problem arises, volunteers should be instructed to call the volunteer coordinator or the campaign manager and have a list of phone numbers to call in an emergency. Everyone on the campaign may have trouble communicating due to the high volume of calls. Any irregularity should be documented. Take photos and get names.

Volunteers should agree to work a specific schedule, preferably all day. Most people come to vote during rush hour: from opening time to 10AM and from 3PM to closing time.

The Finance Director

Be sure to call all your major contributors, thank them for their support, and confirm that they will vote. Get together with your treasurer and find out how many outstanding debts are remaining. Today is your last best chance to raise extra money for the campaign. At the Election Night party, be sure to announce any outstanding debts and pass the hat if necessary.

The Communications Director

The communications director may be the one lead staffer who stays in the office today, especially if you have a phone bank. If no presence in the office is necessary, he or she can work at a precinct. The media should be within easy reach and be able to speak with the communications director all day.

The Election Night Party

All of your friends, family, contributors, volunteers, and supporters should be invited to a party to begin after the polls close. You may decide to have this party at your headquarters, but it is recommended that you reserve a room at a popular bar or restaurant. You may decide to have a party together with other minor party and Independent candidates. This is an especially good idea if multiple candidates are running locally. This increases your chances of media attention. Be sure to thank everyone for their great work.

After the Campaign

Congratulations. You've survived your first roller coaster campaign ride. Take a day off and rest, but there are still some items you need to wrap up before it's all over. Many first-time candidates neglect to properly finish their campaign business. This is a mistake that can lead to indebtedness and fines.

First, meet with your campaign manager and key staff. Determine what bills are outstanding and need to be paid. If you rented an office or equipment, or began telephone, cable, or internet service for the campaign, you will need to end your contracts and service. Take special care to be sure you're up to date and will no longer be charged. All your bills and employees must be paid before you close your account. Carefully keep track of every item in the office and place it in storage or return it to the proper owner. Campaigns often have problems with theft in the last days as volunteers sometimes feel "entitled."

Second, speak with your treasurer, your finance director, and the Elections Office to determine what needs to be done with your campaign's bank account and finances. If you are planning to run for office in the future, you may be able to keep your campaign active. Some public officials decide to keep their campaigns open permanently so they can accept contributions at any time for the next race. Remember that a legally active campaign usually requires reports to be filed by certain deadlines throughout the year, even if there hasn't been any activity. If you want to end your campaign completely, find out all your legal responsibilities from the local Elections Office. Ask about your options for any extra money in your account, or what to do in case of outstanding debts.

Third, take down all your signage before the local deadline and as soon as possible. Your neighbors will be thankful that you've taken care of your signs, and you will avoid any possible fines. Some types of signs and sign posts are re-usable. Save these for your next campaign or donate them to someone else. Gather up all your campaign material, literature, and promotional items. Certain things aren't worth keeping and should be thrown out, but keep some samples of each campaign item for future reference. Try to save anything that might be useful in the future or serve as mementos for your family and friends.

A Win-Win Situation

If you have followed the advice given in this book and by the *I CAN* network, then you are truly a winner. Some battles are won, and some are lost. Whatever happens in your particular campaign, you have won.

You have gained valuable experience that will make you a better candidate or campaign manager for the next time. You found and organized a wonderful team of volunteers who love and respect you. You have found financial contributors who believe in you and can make things happen. The members of your community know that you care about them and that you are a valuable resource if they ever need your help. You have served your country, your state, and your locality with your dedication to a noble cause. Now, you have the opportunity to use all these new resources to continue the fight. The only way that you can lose is if you give up and quit after all this hard work and struggle.

Step 18

Govern Well

The easiest way to be re-elected is to govern well. But that should not be the only reason. The members of your community have placed their lives and livelihoods in your hands. It is your sacred duty to preserve their lives, liberties, and property in an open and accountable government.

I have known many Independent office holders. They have similar stories that can teach us how to govern. Always remember that everyone in a community must learn to work together to achieve great things. If you don't agree with someone, you don't have to be an obnoxious obstacle, and you don't have to compromise your beliefs. The best Independent office-holders find a "third option" that can benefit everyone in a way that grants special favor to no one.

Remember that there are issues in the pro-liberty movement that most people can agree on. Focus your priorities on solving these issues first.

Remember to frame your arguments with the needs of the listeners in mind. Do not pontificate on abstract principles. You have been hired to do a job, not get on a soapbox. You will achieve bigger and better successes with a positive attitude and uplifting spirit.

www.ingramcontent.com/pod-product-compliance
Lightning Source LLC
Chambersburg PA
CBHW072159270326
41930CB00011B/2486